BE THE DOLPHIN

HOW TO LIVE A HEART-CENTERED LIFE

MELINDA MCDONALD PAJAK

MINDCASTLE DESIGNS
SAN DIEGO CA

Copyright © 2017 by Melinda McDonald Pajak

All rights reserved. No part of this publication may be reproduced, distributed or transmitted in any form or by any means, including photocopying, recording, or other electronic or mechanical methods, without the prior written permission of the publisher, except in the case of brief quotations embodied in critical reviews and certain other noncommercial uses permitted by copyright law. For permission requests, write to the publisher, addressed "Attention: Permissions Coordinator," at the address below. Why are you still reading this copyright message? Go. Read the book. Now.
MindCastle Designs
PO Box 34531
San Diego, CA/92103
melindapajak.com
Cover Art ©2017 Debbie Tilley
debbietilley@sbcglobal.net

Ordering Information:
melindapajak.com

Be the Dolphin/ Melinda McDonald Pajak. —1st ed.
ISBN 978-0-9986674-0-9

Contents

Part I: All About Energy 1
   Chapter 1: Introduction 3
   Chapter 2: Underlying Principles 11
   Chapter 3: Happy Energy & Happy People 23
   Chapter 4: Three Energy Modes 43

Part II: Dolphin Behaviors 91
   Chapter 5: Mindfulness 95
   Chapter 6: Heart-Centered Living 107
   Chapter 7: Know Your Values, Identity, & Boundaries 125
   Chapter 8: Practice Gratitude & Identify Beauty 149
   Chapter 9: Engage Intuition & Intention 155
   Chapter 10: Live in Flow & Play in Joy 177
   Chapter 11: Practice Acceptance & Care of Self & Others 185
   Chapter 12: Be Authentic & Open 197
   Chapter 13: Letting Go & Trusting the Universe 205
   Chapter 14: Cooperation Over Competition 209
   Chapter 15: A World of Dolphins 217

Dedication

For Artie and Ben with all my love

"There is nothing in a caterpillar that tells you it's going to be a butterfly."

-R. Buckminster Fuller

PART 1

ALL ABOUT ENERGY

[1]
INTRODUCTION

MY DAD TOLD ME all through my childhood that this world is all made of energy—one energy. He'd say to me, "You have to feeeeeeeel it." He'd ask me if I felt the energy of different places or if I noticed how the breeze felt or how the ocean water felt between my toes. He asked me to feel the energy of all these things. He also used to tell me it's all about balance (well, he still does actually).

These were two concepts placed early on in my head and I am thankful. I began to notice more than just what is on the surface level of things. I know that many times during my adolescence, I rolled my eyes at these philosophical lectures of his but now I am just so grateful. My Mom and Dad chose to expose me to the underlying energy and beauty of this world that I feel in some ways, I am still trying to understand. And maybe I will always continue to seek this understanding. Maybe that's just my journey. So far, it's been great.

I've always been interested in energy. Looking back I see that this has been a passion of mine for many years. I knew when something didn't "feel" right. I had a lot of intuition around "feeeeeeling" things but didn't become more conscious of that fact until later. I began by sorting out these feelings and putting names on them. I began to ferret out what were "my feelings" and what were "other people's feelings." I began to realize that I had been an empath—

taking on everyone else's feelings, good or bad. I took on their stuff and carried it back home with me whether it was anger, frustration, jealousy, or fear. I spent a few years not understanding this while I was working my 9 to 5 job in educational software. I was a roller coaster of emotions because I didn't understand some basic concepts about energy.

My study of energy continued when I took a Feng Shui certificate program at the Western School of Feng Shui with Terah Kathryn Collins when I was 27. It was great fun. I learned all about Chi and how this energy runs through all the objects in your home and through your home. I learned about elemental energy (wood, fire, water, metal, earth) and how to balance them. I was fascinated. I studied this off and on for years. I studied altars and began to keep one on my desk as this grounded my energy. I meditated on and off and visited various churches and centers for spiritual living and checked out the "energy" to see if I wanted to return. My journey of seeking continued.

When I became pregnant in 2002, my intuition kicked in big time. I began getting what I call "psychic" hits about things and then finding out I was right. This was a new way of interacting with energy. And it was exciting because I had always wanted to have extra sensory perception (ESP) when I was a kid. I lost track of this skill post-pregnancy as I was too busy with my newborn son. I was just trying to get some sleep and eat my cold cereal before the baby woke up again. I didn't have enough energy to think about energy. But then a crisis hit. My husband was diagnosed with tonsil cancer when my son was just three months old. Whoa. The health of my love was in jeopardy and it hit me hard, really hard. That was the lowest time of my entire life and I felt like I had no structure or tools or friends to help me out of this tough space. I moved through it with barely enough energy to take care of our son and my husband. There was no time or energy to take care of me. I cried nearly every day as my husband went through two surgeries and then radiation treatment for six weeks. I had no support system. I had no foundation on which to retreat and gain strength and energy to see me through.

I remember my parents had come for the weekend to help me out while my husband had his second surgery. They had just left and were on the freeway back to Orange County. I felt so lost. I was sitting on the floor with my son bawling my eyes out and I felt like I didn't have any strength or belief to hold on to. I called my parents on the road and pleaded with them to come back. I didn't know what else to do.

I don't know if you've ever had an experience like that when you feel so low and you just don't know how you are going to get through the next minute let alone the next day or the next week. I managed somehow to plow through the experience taking care of our little family but one thing was different. I never, ever wanted to go through something like that again feeling so disconnected, isolated, and having no foundation of belief to support me. I needed to find a new way to be in this world that felt stronger and more powerful just in case something else earth shattering were to occur in my life. I couldn't go through what I had just gone through in the same way I had. I wasn't strong enough.

Looking back, this was the push I needed to lay down some foundational beliefs that would support me in times of need. I was driven and even though I was taking care of a small child and a recovering husband (he's been cancer free now for 13 years—yay!), I was going to start putting together a ladder of support for myself. And this is what I am giving to you in this book. I am showing you my ladder of support. It's a ladder that keeps your energy up so you can be happier in your every day life. I've been seeking and doing research and experimenting with what works and what doesn't for these past 13 years and I'm sharing what I've found with you. It is my hope that even just one of you reading this will find this helpful and applicable to your own life. If I can help you avoid even an ounce of the misery I experienced in my darkest moments, then I win. I win big and it would have been worth it.

I have structured this book around three underlying principles and four main points. The three underlying principles are that we are all connected, we are each responsible, and there are two major forces in the universe—love and fear so choose love. This is the scaffolding that supports my ladder of support. If you have not accepted these principles as a part of your life, I ask you now to take a look at each one of them and explore them. I find them to be woven into the fabric of our lives so much so that they cannot be separated from our existence.

The four main points of my book are as follows. I want to clearly transmit this so you can see where this book is going. First, my experience of this world has led me to the conclusion that when you have good amounts of energy, happiness is much more easily achieved. When you don't have enough energy, happiness is harder to access. The second point is the realization that you and only you are responsible for getting and maintaining your energy level. This goes back to the principle that centers on individual responsibility. You are responsible for your energy level and therefore, your happiness.

The third point is that you can achieve optimal energy creation and maintenance by engaging in what I have termed "dolphin behavior" (be the dolphin). This dolphin behavior includes mindfulness, heart-centered living, knowing your values, setting boundaries, practicing gratitude, identifying beauty, engaging intuition and intention, living in flow, practicing acceptance and self-care, being authentic and open, letting go and trusting the universe, and engaging cooperation over competition. The fourth and final point is related to the quote below.

"Changing the world for the better begins with individuals creating inner peace within themselves."- Dalai Llama

When you create inner peace or optimal energy levels inside you, your happiness ripples out. I cite research in this book that supports this and it's also what I intuitively know to be true. By being the dolphin, you exert influence and spread happiness not only to your loved ones but to everyone you come in contact with in your daily life. You literally spread love around when you are living in a heart-centered way. That can only help the world be a better place, right?

That brings me to the why behind the why of writing this book. I look around and I see suffering, loneliness, poverty, war, hatred, destruction of our environment, and racism just to name a few things. For a long time, I didn't know what I could do. How was I going to help? What could really help? I thought about this for a long time—years, in fact. Then a vision came to me during meditation. I saw a world where everyone was heart-centered and helping one another. I saw cooperation. I saw intuition realized into a beautiful flow between human beings. I saw beauty in small tasks done for others. It all came from a heart-centered awareness or way of being in the world.

I had experienced this myself. I knew that when I was heart-centered, I could not make decisions based on ego or greed or hate. I could only make decisions based on what was in the best and highest good of everyone involved. I could only make decisions based on love not fear. Fear cannot occupy the same space as love. This gave me an idea. What if our lawmakers, politicians, and policymakers were required to be heart-centered prior to any action being taken like a vote? Wow. What would that look like? I began to envision a machine that could tell if you were heart-centered or not like a walk-through metal detector that Congress would have to walk through to get to the Senate floor. Or there could be a cuff they would wear when they vote that wouldn't let them vote unless they were heart-centered. My imagination ran away with me but the point remained that if more people were heart-centered, there would be less suffering, loneliness, poverty, war, hatred, destruction of the environment, and racism. If I could help begin to turn the tide towards more people being heart-centered, then maybe, just maybe I could start a ripple that could change the tide of our fear-based world towards one centered in love. Maybe that could be a way for me to make a positive difference. Out of that thought, this book was born.

I thank you for picking up this book and holding it in your hand. It is my intention that even just holding this book will give you a lift—a positive nudge in the direction of heart-centeredness. If this feels good, then take this book home with you now. Read it. Enjoy it. Share it. We need as many heart-centered people as possible right now. The world needs you!

[2]

Underlying Principles

YOU ALL KNOW THE movie, "Star Wars," right? I'm talking about the first one that came out in 1977. I love that movie for so many reasons and I think it deeply impacted my childhood. It was the first time I ever heard of the concept "The Force" and how Obi-Wan Kenobi described it as "an energy field created by all living things. It surrounds us and penetrates us. It binds the galaxy together." Whoa.

There is some sort of energy that connects us all and then you can learn to work with it to become a Jedi? You can even learn to see while you have a blindfold on. That sounded awesome. That was the start of a lifelong journey seeking and exploring topics like extrasensory perception, near death experiences, meditation, and more recently, quantum mechanics, looking for more information on this energy field. It has truly fascinated me since I was seven years old.

I found out more studying some of Einstein's work. I plunged into deeper levels of meditation. I hired a teacher to help develop my intuitive skills. But it wasn't until I read Lynn McTaggart's **The Field** that I could see quantum physics, meditation, and the Force all come together in one interesting congruence of ideas. There has been a lot of research in recent years about quantum physics that tends to support a longstanding spiritual principle that our thoughts, expectations, and intentions affect the physical world around us. In my heart of hearts, I know this to be true. I'm not sure I can explain how but I know it to be true. Having some science meet the field of spirituality is shocking and amazing. I do believe there is much more to our universe and how it works than we will know in many, many lifetimes.

So why can't there be an intersection and a powerful connection between science and spirituality? I do acknowledge that there is another group of scientists upset with spiritual seekers glomming onto this research on subatomic particles and how they behave to prove their point. I understand that. I, in no way, mean to gloss over the scientific results or have the final say on how they should be interpreted. I understand that this field is growing and changing and every day there are new discoveries. I am excited for that. I simply offer that there may be a connection here and leave it up to the reader to interpret, on their own, how these puzzle pieces fit together. Some readers may have never heard of this connection or how the field of quantum physics is even on the same game board as spirituality.

I won't go into too much technical background research on here (and I'm not qualified to do so anyway) so hang in there. Ms. McTaggart, author of **The Field**, interviewed a band of scientists who rethought some equations that had always been subtracted out of quantum physics. She wrote, "These equations stood for the Zero Point Field--an ocean of microscopic vibrations in the space between things. If the Zero Point Field were included in our conception of the most fundamental nature of matter, they realized, the very underpinning of our universe was a heaving sea of energy -- one vast quantum field. If this were true, everything would be connected to everything else like some invisible web." (McTaggart, 2008) That sounds a lot like the concept of the Force from Star Wars.

What I find most fascinating is that McTaggart went on to state, "On our most fundamental level, living beings, including human beings, were packets of quantum energy constantly exchanging information with this inexhaustible energy sea." (McTaggart, 2008) Reread that last sentence. WE are packets of energy exchanging information with a sea of energy. So, we're interacting with the sea of energy around us or "the Force." That Force is in us, next to us, around us, and interacting with us all the time. What a notion. Have you thought about that before? What are the implications of that? If we are each a packet of energy and our best friend is also a packet of energy, what happens between us when we get angry or give each other a hug? What does the sea of energy do? What happens to the energy in our individual packets? Does it increase? Does it decrease? Does one person get more energy than the other?

In **The Celestine Prophecy**, the author, James Redfield, uses an engaging story to share spiritual insights and the Third Insight is related to this concept of energy all around us. One of the characters explains, "In other words, the basic stuff of the universe, at its core, is looking like a kind of pure energy that is malleable to human intention and expectation in a way that defies our old mechanistic model of the universe—as though our expectation itself causes our energy to flow out into the world and affect other energy systems." (Redfield, 1993) The main character goes on to explore an old growth forest and sees these energy fields for himself much to his amazement.

So if we could see the energy around us and between us and inside of us, what would that look like? What would it feel like? What would we be more aware of? There is so much more going on around us than our previous scientific researchers have shown us. Some scientists are getting closer to revealing what is going on and we'll go over some of that. But we also need to feel our way through this understanding of how the world works. Sometimes we dismiss what we can't see because we haven't been able to scientifically test it and prove it to be true. Do we need a scientist to tell us love exists? Don't we feel that with our heart, our soul, our entire being?

If you really want to study energy, it's best to start with a scientist most people have heard of and who, after all, came up with a way to measure energy in his famous equation, $E=mc^2$. On my path, I read many of Einstein's thoughts on everything from love to the universe and I was surprised at the depth and beauty in this man. This particular passage by him is quite intriguing. "A human being is a part of the whole, called by us 'Universe,' a part limited in time and space. He experiences himself, his thoughts and feelings as something separated from the rest—a kind of optical delusion of his consciousness. The striving to free oneself from this delusion is the one issue of true religion. Not to nourish the delusion but to try to overcome it is the way to reach the attainable measure of peace of mind." (Einstein, 1950) This all points to the first principle this book is based on which is we are all connected.

A. WE ARE ALL CONNECTED

Spiritual seekers usually begin with the idea that we are all connected by an energy whether you call it the Force, the universe, God, or Goddess, it doesn't matter. The idea of us all being connected has been around for thousands of years in spiritual or religious thought but to hear it written about from one of the world's leading scientists in the 20th century is something else altogether. I like to think of the image of the Tree of Life where we are all leaves on the tree of humanity sharing one planet as we share the trunk and branches that support us in our time on this planet. And when our time is done, we shrivel and drop from the tree back to the earth to nurture and support the tree until it is our time to be reborn as a new leaf. And the cycle of life continues.

This idea of connection between all of humanity is one of the underlying principles of spirituality and of this book. Understanding that we are all on the same roller coaster ride of this big blue planet twirling around the sun is critical to being able to receive the rest of the wisdom presented in this book. We are all brothers and sisters born from the same Earth and Sun. What you do to your neighbor, you also do to your self. Most of the world's religions contain the Golden Rule (do unto others as you would have done unto you) and there is a very good reason for that. We were born with an innate knowing that this is true. Our ancestors knew it and many of us walking the earth now have conveniently chosen to forget or ignore it for any number of reasons. It is time now to remember this and cherish it as a spiritual truth. We are in this together. Embracing this will help us face what is next for us as a species. We all play a part in how we move forward so let's walk in cooperation. It's so much easier.

In the book, **Connected: The Surprising Power of Our Social Networks and How They Shape Our Lives,** authors, Nicholas A. Christakis and James H. Fowler, describe their research that supports this notion that we are indeed all connected. Our social networks have a profound effect on us, more so than we ever conceived of before. They researched the contagiousness of things like suicide, obesity, and happiness with intriguing results. Christakis and Fowler wrote, "Our unavoidable embeddedness in social networks means that events occurring in other people—whether we know them or not—can ripple through the network and affect us. A key factor in determining our health is the health of others. We are affected not only by the health and behavior of our partners and friends but also by the health and behavior of hundreds or thousands of people in our extended social network." (Christakis & Fowler, 2009) So what can explain this? If there were an underlying energy field that we are all connected to, then it would make sense that ripples in this field would make their way to us. And it would make sense that the closer these ripples originate to where we are, the more effected we would be. McTaggart argues "We will notice the ripple effect of every action on an entire chain of being—the living things, the natural world, the friends along the network, the members of our community, the people from other countries whom we benefit or harm by what we do." (McTaggart, The Bond: How to Fix Your Falling-Down World, 2011) (Weiner, 1985) We are all connected in this field of energy and we feel every ripple that goes ou

B. WE ARE EACH RESPONSIBLE

This moves us to the next underlying principle for the wisdom in this book. Just to review, spiritual truth #1 is that we are all connected. Spiritual truth #2 is that we are each responsible for what we bring to this planet, to each other, and to ourselves. Each one of us is responsible for our own happiness and what we contribute to our loved ones, our communities, our species, and our planet. We get to decide if our contribution will be a positive one or a negative one. We have the freedom to choose daily what we will create in our lives and in the lives of those around us. There is no else to blame.

We have control over ourselves and make an impression on those we live near. There is no else to blame if you are not happy or if you are being a negative person who brings everyone else down or if you live from greed and stomp on others to get what you want. There is no one to blame for your own thoughts, words, and actions. These are the gifts given to every person on earth. It is up to you to own them and be responsible for them. Your words and actions can be exquisitely beautiful and life changing. Your words and actions can bring you happiness, love, and bliss. Your words and actions can lift souls and change lives for the better. It is all up to you. Owning that responsibility is an important step in continuing on in this book for maximum retention of the wisdom presented.

Taking responsibility for one's life can be difficult because you have to let go of blaming others. It's a big responsibility that takes a while to get used to. I remember realizing this when I was in my 20's. There was a moment of choice where I had to decide how to move forward. I knew if I took responsibility for my own happiness, there was a much better chance of actually getting there but I also had to let go of being lazy and blaming others. I had to enter into a new way of being that I didn't know how to do. I was not sure where this path led. What if I didn't do a good job with that responsibility? That's an interesting question, right? Well, whom can you blame? You can only blame yourself for being miserable and lost while you pick yourself up off the ground and begin again with renewed purpose.

I remembered a textbook, **Human Motivation**, written by my Psychology Professor at UCLA, Bernard Weiner, who wrote about motivation and locus of control. That went a long way to explaining just how this taking responsibility for one's life worked exactly. This was no spiritual mumbo jumbo (although I'm a big fan of spiritual mumbo jumbo when it feels authentic). This was real research with statistics. Dr. Weiner's Attribution Theory states that "a person's attribution for success or failure determines the amount of effort the individual will expend on the task." (Weiner, 1985)

My professor was looking at the link between motivation and behavior attribution. I promise this will get linked up to taking responsibility for your own happiness in a minute. Dr. Weiner approached motivation from three categories: stable theory, locus of control, and controllability. He was looking at how a person's perceptions of why something went well or why something failed as to how likely they were to try it again. If the person attributed the success AND the failure to things that are within their control or things they can change, they will be much more likely to try that thing again.

For example, a young woman prepares for a dance competition and two nights before, she goes out with her friends, drinks alcohol, and stays up too late. She also misses an important dance practice the next morning as a result. The woman does not win the dance competition. How does she attribute the failure to win? Is it the fault of the judges? Is it the fault of her dance teacher, her choreographer, or her friends for taking her out? If she chooses to attribute her failure to one or more of these people, do you think it's likely that she will enter another dance competition or be really motivated to work hard and win? She is placing the blame outside of herself. She is giving away her control. She is not taking responsibility for why this happened when she blames others.

Now what if she attributes her failure to win to the fact that she partied too much, missed a dance practice, and just didn't have focus with her body and mind? Or maybe she didn't give it her all or practice enough. This would mean she is placing the locus of control on an internal factor. In other words, she is placing responsibility on a factor that she can control. She is willing to look at the possibility that she did not give her best performance. In recognizing that she may be responsible for the failure, she is in a better mental state to get motivated to win next time. She will take steps to make sure she is in better physical and mental preparedness for the next competition. She will work hard and practice more and then see what happens. These actions are within her control so she feels more positive towards entering another dance competition.

If you always feel that your happiness is in the hands of others or in the hands of fate, how willing or motivated will you be to change anything in your life? In the willingness to accept responsibility for who you are, where you are, and what's going on in your life right now, you will automatically have a greater motivation (and freedom) to change it. You will retake control over the outcome of your life and feel empowered to do so. Take back the responsibility you have given to life events, other people, and circumstances beyond your control. This is your life. This is your responsibility and with that responsibility comes the opportunity for the best life possible full of love, light, happiness, and contentment.

C. Choosing Love Over Fear

There are two forces in the universe. They are love and fear. Everything boils down to one of these two forces. Just like there is good and evil, there is love and fear. You must decide which one you will embrace for your life. Which one will be the bottom line for how you live your life? Love is acceptance, joy, happiness, freedom, connection, cooperation, generosity, and peace. Fear is anger, war, violence, hatred, greed, jealousy, judgment, and separation.

I wonder sometimes if we realize how much fear is around us in our own culture. The news media is built on getting you to watch out of fear. If you don't know something, it might kill you. The commercials are structured much the same way. If you don't use this product, you or your children might die. Politicians use the rhetoric of fear in the same way. Vote for me or your way of life will be forever doomed. Do you see that? Do you see how we are manipulated by fear in our every day life? If you can clearly make love your bottom line and connect to the energy of love, you cannot fall into fear or be manipulated by it. This will change the world. Do you see that? If we govern ourselves through love, there is no room for fear. There is no room for manipulation. If we make the bottom line of the world love, there is no greed, no corruption, no secrets, and no fear.

It's all about the choice we make in life. Do we want to base those choices on fear? Or do we want to base those choices on love? The outcomes will directly reflect what you based those choices on.

A year after I finished at UCLA, I was working at the Buckminster Fuller Institute in Los Angeles as an Administrative Assistant making $10 an hour. It was tough to live on that amount and my parents helped me out some. Even though I enjoyed the job, I knew this was not where I wanted to be. One day at work, a friend of the

Institute came by to show us this new interactive CD-ROM called Columbus. This was the beginning of interactive anything and I was blown away. Once I saw that, I knew I wanted to be a part of creating things like that. I asked some questions and got turned on to the field of Educational Technology (using technology to teach). I went to the UCLA Resource Center and looked up any certificate or degree programs in that specific field. I found a promising one at San Diego State University. I called them up and found out more about the program and had them send me additional information. The woman said I could start in the fall if I wanted to. This was May.

It was at this point that I had a choice. I could stay in L.A. and work in a low paid position, which was steady, interesting, but going nowhere. Or I could take a risk and move to San Diego and begin a Master's program that might lead me to a meaningful career doing something that excited me. I could choose to make a decision based on love—love of what I wanted to do for a career and the excitement that comes with that. Or I could choose to make a decision based on fear—fear that I won't like the Master's program, fear that I won't like San Diego, fear that I didn't know anyone and would have to make friends all over again, fear of moving to a new city, and the fear of not finding a new job to help support myself. There was a lot to fear but I chose to base my decision on love. I had an intuitive knowing in my heart that this was the right move. I knew, somehow, that I would meet a man and that I belonged in San Diego earning a Master's degree. I felt like my life would fall into place once I got there. I took a leap of faith based on love and it all worked out.

I found an apartment fairly quickly near the beach, which I loved. I enjoyed my classes and met my future husband within three weeks of moving to San Diego. I got my Master's degree two years later and we married a year after that. I've been living in San Diego ever since and enjoyed the career I had using that degree as a jumping off point. What if I had chosen to stay in L.A. out of fear? How different would my life have been? What would have happened? I can't say for sure. But I do know I followed the trail marked LOVE not FEAR and it worked out extremely well for me.

In this book, I attempt to show you how to make love your bottom line for making decisions that affect every part of your life for the better. If you want more acceptance, joy, happiness, freedom, connection, and cooperation and you feel that we are connected and you are ready to take responsibility for your own life, then read on and enjoy.

[3]

Happy Energy & Happy People

WHEN DO YOU FEEL happiest? When something amazing happens to you, how do you feel? What is your energy level when that happens? Have you ever thought about it?

When you feel happy, your energy level is naturally high. And the opposite is true as well. When you are sad, angry, or frustrated, your energy is really, really low. When you are in the midst of being angry, you can have an influx of quick energy but it drains you quickly.

Do you think you can be your best self when your energy is low? Think of a day where some things went wrong and you were low emotionally and physically. On that day, do you think you would be playful, quick to laugh, compassionate towards someone who was angry, or forgive someone his or her mistakes from this place of low energy? Do you think you could be a good parent or a well-behaved child if you were feeling really low on energy?

If we had lots of happy energy, would we be better friends, lovers, co-workers, parents, sisters, brothers, aunts, uncles, grandparents, or even kids? Yes. This is a very common pitfall especially among parents—lack of energy. When we have more energy we are more likely to take an extra minute to answer our child's incessant questions or laugh about the spilled milk or give an extra hug or word of encouragement, right? But it is true for all us no matter what role we play in each other's lives. When you have more energy, you are just that much more likely to be your best self.

I love the work done by Doc Childre and Howard Martin at the HeartMath Institute. From their book, **The HeartMath Solution**, they write, "The way we accumulate and spend our vital energy reserves is the primary factor that determines the quality of our lives. Most of us aren't used to associating our emotions with our energy level. We may be vaguely aware that when we're enthusiastic, our energy goes way up. But how often do we associate the emotions we've experienced with how tired we feel at the end of the day?" (Childre, Martin, & Beech, 1999)

We think more clearly, we are more in touch with our emotions, and we can find a more balanced sense of ourselves when we have energy. Would that be worth a little effort each day? Would you like to be happier on a daily basis? Would you like to know how?

I came across this quote from an aquatic biologist at Swansea University in the UK named Rory Wilson who wrote, 'If animals are going to collect one thing that's analogous to money, it's energy." (Wilson, 2014) I find that intriguing. To animals, energy is equal to money. And really money is equal to energy, right? Energy is our common coin in this universe. The more we have energy, the richer we are. We are animals too. Does that make you a bit more interested in gaining more energy? If you think about energy as money, that might give you additional motivation.

So what if you knew some ways to get a happy energy boost quickly and easily while in the car or at the park or in line at the grocery store? What if you understood some ways that your happy energy gets stolen from you throughout your day and you learned ways to counteract that? What if you could protect your happy energy like you do your purse or your cell phone? Do you think that might change how you show up as a parent, a co-worker, or a friend? Do you think you might be happier to boot? Happiness comes more easily when you learn to own your energy and protect it.

A.   The MegaEnergyTron

Let's start at the beginning. We are all made up of energy. We are made up of cells that are made up of atoms that are made up of tiny electrons, protons, and neutrons and all of that is energy. We feel this energy running through our body. It's what makes us alive. We see energy in our puppy as he races around the house or in our child when he is playing baseball or in our lemon tree when it flowers and produces fruit. We see energy in the wind in the trees and in the sunlight shining down and in the ocean waves. It is all around us. It is in us. This energy permeates the universe.

Now the energy level inside of you is distinct although not separate. Your personal energy can go up or down depending on what is going on in your life. When you are sad, frustrated, or sick, those energy levels can feel way low. When you are happy and feel on top of the world, your energy level can feel super high like it's overflowing and you'd happily dance all the way down the street. What makes that happen?

Well, I've thought about and studied energy a lot—for at least thirty years. My Dad started me down this path of thinking about energy when I was just a kid. He started telling me that everything is energy. It took me a long time to actually listen to him and begin to understand what he was talking about. And after much thought and research, I decided he was right about this. It **is** all about energy and about balancing and maintaining that energy. I've found this to be even more important as I've gotten older.

Childre and Martin in their book, **The HeartMath Solution**, dive into this idea and back it all up with research and experimentation. They wrote "Whether we like it or not, we're accountable for our energy expenditures….We wake up in the morning with a certain amount of vital energy to expend each day. It's up to us whether we expend it in efficient or nonefficient thoughts, feelings, and attitudes." (Childre, Martin, & Beech, 1999)

I wanted a fun way to explain this to my son so I created the idea of the MegaEnergyTron. You see each person has his or her own MegaEnergyTron that regulates his or her energy. I think of it as a little robot inside of our chest. It acts as a gauge to help you monitor your energy level. Learning to understand and use your own personal MegaEnergyTron is critical for happiness and contentment in life.

Understanding the different types of energy, how to maintain energy, and how one can lose energy while interacting with others allows you to regulate and personalize your own MegaEnergyTron. You personalize it by gathering the processes that work for YOU to raise up and stabilize your energy (this is the experimentation aspect noted by Childre and Martin). It's important to recognize that this is different for each person and that's why you have your own customized MegaEnergyTron.

I think about energy in terms of a big gauge on the front of your MegaEnergyTron. Throughout each day, we need to look at our energy gauge to see how we're doing. Becoming aware of our energy level is the first step in becoming more mindful. Our energy level moves up and down all day long because we are emotional and physical animals living a life in this physical world. It's fine for our energy levels to move along a continuum but if you begin to pay attention to your energy, you can start to fine-tune your days so the energy remains on the higher end of that continuum. And do you know what happens when you do that? You are happier and ultimately, a better human being. I know this because I started to do it regularly—every day and it has made a huge difference to my family and me. I became the ripple of happiness in our family pond and that ripple continues out to an even larger community pond.

If you start checking your energy gauge during the day and become aware that your energy is low, how do you get more of it? How do you raise your energy levels to where you can be happy again? Where does energy come from? Does it come from other people? Or where? Did you know that some people take other people's energy? Have you had energy taken from you? The thing is—we are all energy beings. We all want energy. The good news is that there is plenty of energy to go around. There is a limitless supply that you can access easily—thank goodness.

B. TYPES OF ENERGY

In my experience and my study of energy, I have found it easier to divide energy into different types. There are four types that are helpful for this discussion: Personal, Group/Situational, Foundational, and Universal.

The first type of energy is already very familiar to you and it's **PERSONAL** energy. This is the energy of an individual. You can picture a big bubble of energy around a person and that is her energy field. Rollin McCraty, a researcher, writes in his paper "The heart generates the largest electromagnetic field in the body. The electrical field is measure in an electrocardiogram (ECG) is about 60 times greater in amplitude than the brain waves recorded in an electroencephalogram (EEG)." (McCraty, 2004) He shares that this magnetic field can be measured several feet away from the body. We each clearly have our own personal energy field that is measurable. Is it really so strange then that when you first meet someone, you can literally "feel" their energy? This energy evaluation, most often completed on a subconscious level, provides us with a first impression.

Let's focus then on your individual personal energy field. Did you know that you are the one in control of the energy in this field? Let me make that a statement. You are in control of your own energy field—always and in every way. This is one of the true strengths of becoming more aware of your energy field or your MegaEnergyTron. When you accept that you are in control of your own energy, you take responsibility for it. This changes everything. You now realize that you own your energy field and you can reset it anytime. There is a big red RESET button just below the energy gauge on your MegaEnergyTron. You can use this RESET button at any time. We'll cover this more later on.

You determine whether your energy is up or down or if you let someone or some situation take all of your energy. You determine whether you want to fill up your energy reserve and reset yourself. It is up to you. This is the first type of enerThe second type of energy is **GROUP** or **SITUATIONAL** energy. We recognize this energy whenever we attend an event like a political rally, a rock concert, the ballet, or even a Major League Baseball game. There is a distinct ball of energy formed by all the people there, the intention set by the event organizers, and the expectation of the people going to the event. If all the people at the rock concert want loud, rocking music and a great time, that will be the energy of the event. If all the ballet goers, want a quiet, moving expression of humanity in dance, that will be the energy of the event. But the people attending must also carry that intention or it can move in a different direction.

You can tune into this energy and get more out of the event if your intention and expectation are in alignment with the **GROUP** energy. It can be an amazing experience. But GROUP energy can also be dark, violent, and chaotic. Think of any kind of protest that turned violent with groups of people burning cars and looting stores. It's important to understand this type of energy because it can be used in amazingly positive ways or in destructive ways. Energy is just energy. It's neutral. How it's used or focused is what matters.

FOUNDATIONAL energy is an interesting type of energy that sets the direction for a family, home, business, organization, or location.

Many businesses have a mission statement and I've seen many employees roll their eyes at this but I believe it's very important. Setting this type of intention can be beneficial for other groups as well.

Mission statements set the foundational energy for a business and this is important energetically. People recognize energy on a subconscious level and if they walk into a small business like a coffee shop and there is a mishmash of foundational energy along with all the personal energies of the people that work there, it might not be as pleasant or welcoming as it could because there is no clarity to the intention of the business. When the employees, the boss, and the intention or foundational energy are all in alignment, there is clarity and a positive feeling about the business. This is palpable and you can feel it when you walk into a restaurant and no one is there and it feels weird. Yes, that is the foundational energy that is not clear or in alignment. The ice cream shop that always has a line out the door and has a positive vibe has an excellent foundational energy. The energy and intentions are in alignment and are transmitting clearly to everyone within "feeling" distance.

One thing to think about for the future is how you can use the power of foundational energy to enhance your own family. You can write a mission statement for your family setting the foundation for how you want your family to work, be, and live. There are some exercises coming up where you can practice this.

Another example of this is Disneyland. They advertise their mission statement all the time as the "Happiest Place on Earth." That is the **FOUNDATIONAL** energy for their amusement parks. The employees are encouraged to make every visitor's experience there a happy one (I know because I used to work there a long, long time ago). The feel of the amusement park backstage and in the park IS happy—there is alignment among the employees and the intention of the happiest place on earth. Even the customers engage and repeat this mantra of the happiest place on earth. This creates even more alignment and energy towards that end. They clearly transmit the experience of going to their amusement park and obviously it has worked well.

Lots of joy happens there. I'm not plugging Disneyland but simply pointing out how setting an intention or mission statement can drive and plant the FOUNDATIONAL energy for a location. Disneyland is just a great example of this.

So, where does all this energy come from? Well, I call it **UNIVERSAL** energy. It's where we all came from. It's what we are all made of. We are all bits of space dust. Neil deGrasse Tyson describes it this way: "We are part of this universe; we are in this universe, but perhaps more important than both of those facts, is that the universe is in us." (Tyson) Once we understand and become aware that UNIVERSAL energy is all around us, we can consciously connect to it and replenish our supply should we run low. UNIVERSAL energy is in all the plants, animals, clouds, mountains, and so on all around us. Just think of it as The Force.

I think of **UNIVERSAL** energy as a giant gas station in the sky where we can fill up our **PERSONAL** energy containers (our MegaEnergyTrons) anytime we want. There are many ways to connect to this gas station in the sky. You could meditate for a few minutes and get connected and filled up. Or for another person, it might be a walk in nature that fills them up. Just understanding that it's possible to fill up on **UNIVERSAL** energy is a huge step forward in accepting responsibility for your own energy and therefore, your own happiness. It all comes back to your MegaEnergyTron. You need to realize you have one and then take responsibility for keeping it in good working order. When your energy is up, then guess what? You are happy. And when you are happy, your children, your spouse, your neighbors, your co-workers, and so on are happier too and the world is a better place.

C. MINDFULNESS

One of the leaders of the mindfulness movement is Jon Kabat-Zinn who described mindfulness as "an openhearted, moment-to-moment, non-judgmental awareness." (Kabat-Zinn, 2005) Kabat-Zinn believes that mindfulness is best cultivated through meditation. Just so you know, meditation does not have to be a five hour-long religious experience tied to an ashram in India or a Buddhist temple in Tibet. It's not that there is anything wrong with that but I want you to separate meditation from a religious practice. Meditation is not necessarily a religious tool. It's a tool for all human beings regardless of your religious beliefs. So is the practice of being mindful.

You may have heard the word "mindfulness" being discussed around sports. If you believe a big part of sports is the mental game then you will understand why having your mind focused and relaxed is critical for an excellent performance. I remember hearing about how the Chicago Bulls and Michael Jordan took on meditation as a part of their basketball practice to enhance their performance. George Mumford, the man who taught meditation to the Chicago Bulls, says "When they are playing their best, they can do no wrong, and no matter what happens they are always a step quicker, a step ahead. That happens when we are in the moment, when we are mindful of what is going on." (Gordhamer, 2011)

It is an awareness of the present moment. Sports psychology researchers have sat up and taken notice of mindfulness and how it may affect performance of athletes. In a study on "Mindfulness and Acceptance Approaches in Sport Performance," researchers found that the golfers who were trained in mindfulness and acceptance, played better, enhanced their national ranking, and met their competition goals. "They [the mindful golfers] generally stated that they had developed skills with reference to attentional awareness; a nonjudgmental, task-relevant attentional focus; and behavioral flexibility." (Bernier, Thienot, Codron, & Fournier, 2009)

That all sounds great but how do you get there? What is mindfulness exactly? Well, when you are mindful, you are observing thoughts and feelings you are having without judgment. It's all about being aware.

In relation to the MegaEnergyTron, we have talked about how important being aware of your energy level is and this is the first part of mindfulness. Mindfulness is important because it helps you figure out when your energy is low allowing an impetus for you to take action and fix it.

1. THREE MINDFULNESS STEPS
    a. **STOP** -You have to stop and give yourself a moment to get mindful. (Remind yourself that you have a MegaEnergyTron)
    b. **OBSERVE** -Observe yourself to identify your energy level and notice your thoughts and feelings without judgment. (Read the gauge on your MegaEnergyTron)
    c. **RESET** -Reset your energy level and thoughts through taking action. (Hit the RESET button on your MegaEnergyTron)

Sometimes just becoming aware of where you are during a state of mindfulness automatically begins the process of pushing your own Reset button. But it's important to know what works best for you in terms of resetting your energy. Is it a breathing exercise, a meditation, or a walk in the park? It's good to have a whole bag of reset button practices that you can pull from although generally, I prefer meditation over almost anything else. It works every time for me.

Most mindfulness practices recommend meditation as your go to reset practice. If you meditate on a regular basis, you can develop quicker reset actions. A quick reset can be three deep breaths and thinking a happy thought. Your happy thought could be a wonderful memory where you felt peaceful and happy. It has to be a very strong memory or maybe a place that brings forth these feelings. Focus on that and do three deep breaths. Having a fast way to reset can be important in this busy physical world.

For example, if you are meeting at the playground for a get together with your toddler and 5 other kids and their moms, sitting down for a 20 minute meditation is just crazy talk. A better option might be the three breaths and a happy thought practice mentioned above. Or since you are outside, maybe you could focus your awareness on the beauty of the trees and the grass while reflecting on what you are grateful for while keeping one eye trained on your child.

Developing a mindfulness practice is all about experimentation and finding what works for you. Regular meditation is a sure fire way to make a mindfulness practice easier to engage in on a moment's notice.

2.   PAUSE BUTTON

Our lives are so busy and full and our society pushes us to do more, be more, etc. We need to take responsibility to slow ourselves down and use the PAUSE button (also located on your MegaEnergyTron). When you begin to practice mindfulness on a more regular basis and have been checking in with your MegaEnergyTron, you may notice that there is a space between a thought and an action. Allowing for this space between thought and action is critical to protecting our energy and keeping ourselves happy. When you slow down, you see that before every action you take, there is a space or a pause where you have a choice to take that action. It's as if time slows down and you notice this space and this choice. This is the PAUSE button.

You can begin to notice this space and consciously press the PAUSE button so that you can better examine your choices in this moment before you take action. With time and practice, you can use this PAUSE button more effectively and make better choices. This may seem obvious but when you realize how important your thoughts are, you want to slow down and make sure that what you are thinking is in alignment with your intentions and that the action you are thinking about taking will help get you there. Taking a moment to ponder your choices leads to better decision-making and more happiness in your life.

When we don't think or pause, we are rushed and are open to the influences around us in that moment. We may not be in alignment with that quiet voice inside us that tries to help us make the best decisions for our best and highest good. Next time you feel rushed to make a decision, hit the PAUSE button. Take a moment to think clearly and breathe. Practice mindfulness for a minute and make a better choice that is in alignment with who you are and where you want to go. You'll be glad you did.

I know that I used to get rattled quite often with making decisions in the moment. I might be faced with a group of friends or in a meeting where I am asked to make a choice to do something and I feel under pressure. I would often just blurt out "Yes, of course." When in actuality, I had not thought about it and couldn't even figure out in the moment if this was something I wanted to do. I might have been feeling ungrounded or flooded with the energies of others around me making it impossible for me to answer with integrity. When that happens, I find it difficult to tune into my own wants and desires (said as a true recovering people pleaser).

Instead of blurting out an answer like I have done in the past, I have learned to take a pause. I just take a moment and pause. Try to listen. And if you can, ask to get back to that group of friends or the people in the meeting with your answer in a little while. Give yourself space and time to provide an answer that is in alignment with who you are and where you want to go. Allow yourself the gift of the PAUSE. This allows you to give an answer you won't resent or backpedal on. It allows you to give an answer that is full of integrity and positive energy backed by who you are. Other people will appreciate this and by holding this boundary of needing time to think, you are giving others in that group, permission to do the same. That is a good thing.

Mindfulness is a path for YOU to discover. Learning how your RESET and PAUSE buttons work on YOUR MegaEnergyTron is super important. You can begin to understand your own unique requirements for a state of mindfulness because what works for you may not work for someone else. Maybe you like yoga and someone else needs to take a five-mile run and another needs to play with his dog in order to get more centered and mindful. Does it matter how we get our energy back up? No. It just matters that we replenish our personal energy stores so we can go back to creating a happy, soul-satisfying experience for ourselves. This is a daily and sometimes minute-by-minute practice. This watching the energy gauge on our MegaEnergyTron and hitting the Reset button may happen every hour or once a day depending on where we are and what we are doing. It's a constant practice and one I continue to work on daily.

3. THE HAMSTER BALL

The best way for me to explain the Happy state on the MegaEnergyTron to someone is to use a hamster ball analogy. Have you ever seen a hamster ball—the clear plastic ball that you put your hamster in so he can roll around on the floor? I like to think of our MegaEnergyTron as emitting a clear energy field around us that can appear like a plastic ball around us. When you start your day and you are healthy and have had a good night's sleep, the energy field being emitted by the MegaEnergyTron is strong and at 100%.

Your night of sleep has reset your energy level and you are ready for your day. But what happens over the course of your day? Does your energy level remain at 100%? Does your protective energy field stay as strong as it was when you woke up?

Let's walk through a pretend day and see what happens.

You slept through your alarm. You wake up fifteen minutes late. You run to your child's room to start waking him up so you can get out the door on time. You notice your child has a runny nose. You get him dressed and ready to go wiping his nose and hoping it won't turn into a full-fledged cold. Energy check—your energy started at 100% but has probably dropped down to 95% due to this small stressor. A few minutes later and you are out the door and into the car.

You get to preschool and your child is getting cranky and doesn't want to go inside. You were trying to rush him before and now he really doesn't want to get out of the car seat. And he definitely does not want to walk calmly through the front door. You struggle with your son in tow—half dragging him inside while you are constantly speaking encouraging words in a high squealed, energetic voice. Despite your best efforts, a full-fledged tantrum ensues in front of all the parents at drop off just inside the door.

Now stop for a moment. What do you think is happening to your MegaEnergyTron? What does the gauge say as you walk back to your car? How is that energy field now? Well, it's as if your child had a gigantic Slurpee straw shoved into your perfectly nice hamster ball of energy and has happily sucked out 20% of your energy store just during drop-off. Wow. Your energy has come down from 95% to about 75%. See how that works?

You continue with your day only to arrive late to work. Your boss strides angrily into your office before you even put your purse away. She demands the report that she was promised yesterday. You tell her you'll get it to her as soon as possible. She storms out of your office and you sigh. Once again, what do you think your MegaEnergyTron gauge reads now? It's as if now your boss had another straw in your hamster ball of energy and managed to squeeze out another 15% of your entire day's energy store. Your new grand total is about 60% on the gauge. How do you think you would feel at this moment? How is your day going so far?

At lunchtime, your mother calls complaining that you never visit her and that she misses her grandchild. You feel guilty and think to yourself that you are not being a good daughter. Your energy falls again—15% sucked out by the your mom's straw in your hamster ball. You are now at a meek 45%. Yipes.

On a positive note, you decide to put on your tennis shoes and take a walk after lunch and listen to some music. It feels good to be in nature and doing something physical. Before you know it, you are back up 30% on your energy gauge (75%). Later in the afternoon, a friend calls with great news to share with you and your energy gauge pops up to 80%. And this continues up and down throughout your day.

It is so important to realize that you get to choose how you react in these situations. Let me repeat that. **YOU CHOOSE** whether to give up energy to those seeking to draw it out of you. This is your choice. We talked about the PAUSE button and you can use that in these situations. Pause before you give away your energy. We'll go over this more in the next section. Remember you also get to choose to push the RESET button whenever you want to raise your energy.

How many things do you do for yourself to raise the energy on your MegaEnergyTron? How many times does it seem like your energy just gets obliterated? By the time you go to pick up your child after work, what does your energy gauge read? Do you have any energy left when you have to make dinner, give your child a bath, play with them, and put them to bed? Or maybe you are going to volunteer at a homeless shelter or attend a board meeting for a non-profit or go out for a friend's birthday? How will you show up for these events after a day like that? Is it any wonder so many of us are exhausted when our head hits the pillow?

Have you thought about these energy ups and downs before? What can you do to pump up your own happy energy level? If you haven't been careful about your energy throughout the day, it will affect your evening. How do you think it will affect your interactions with your spouse, your family, your friends, or even with yourself?

Being mindful of the energy gauge on your MegaEnergyTron can be the best way to improve all of your relationships and boost the chance of happiness that can be found each and every day. Understanding how your energy affects your life from moment to moment helps you start taking responsibility for it. And from there, you can start to become more aware and reset your energy whenever you need or want to. A high-energy gauge equals a happy life.

4. WHERE IS YOUR HEAD? ACTIVITY

It can be very helpful to think about where your thoughts go throughout your day. If you tend toward worrying, angry, resentful, or fearful thoughts, your energy will get depleted quickly. If you self-correct those thoughts and focus on the present, you can alleviate some of that energy drain. Where do you spend your thoughts during the day? When you look out the window or are driving somewhere or sitting at your kid's music lesson, what do you think abouTrack your thoughts for a day to see where you are spending the most time. Take a thought and determine whether it is based in love or fear. There are only two forces in the universe and they are love and fear. You get to choose where you focus your thoughts. During the day while you are driving or zoning out, where do you thoughts go? Take notice. This is an important part of mindfulness. Don't judge your thoughts just notice them. Just begin to become aware as to the nature of these thoughts.

After engaging in more mindful activities, I became aware of the thoughts I had and noticed I spent a great deal of time running through "What if" scenarios that were quite upsetting. I had not even realized I was doing it. I would think while I was in the shower, well, what if an attacker came in to the bathroom, how would I defend myself? To this day, I do not know where those thoughts came from. Gradually, with attention, I turned off the habit of doing this and freed my brain up to think more positively about what I was going to do that day or visualize myself as a New York Times bestselling author on a book tour. That was much more beneficial for my blood pressure and me. See if you can be an observer of your own thoughts throughout the day. Be a fly on the wall in your own mind and without judgment, just notice what is going on.

Do your thoughts contain worry, shame, guilt, hate, resentment, anger, or fear? Write down the thought and check the Fear column. Try to list how long was spent on this thought. Did you have some thoughts about love, positive relationships, beauty, art, gratitude, appreciation, recognition, joy, laughter, or connection? Then write those down and check the Love column and list how long you spent thinking about that.

You don't have to spend long on this activity to understand the reasoning behind it. We have never been asked to seriously observe the insides of our heads. What old recordings do we keep playing over and over? Do we have negative self-talk or judgment of others or a deep appreciation of the weather and beauty of the day? What is going on in there? This is a great exercise for discovering and observing all that goes on between your ears. Then, the good news is that you can change it. Yay! You get to choose what chatter and thoughts are floating past in your conscious mind. And you can choose love over fear every time and when you do this, your energy bubble stays at 100%. You may want to start a small notebook with these categories on it so you can keep track.

Where Is Your Head Chart

Thought	Love √	Fear √	Time Spent On This Thought
It's a beautiful day.	√		1 minute
I'm always late. I hate being late.		√	20 minutes
I hate how overweight I am.		√	15 minutes
I love talking and laughing with co-workers.	√		5 minutes

5. ENERGY AWARENESS ACTIVITY

It's important to know which activities, situations, and people contribute or drain your daily energy. Think carefully about how you spend your time and begin to notice whether your energy is up or down after each activity, outing, or person you spend time with. Keep a daily chart for a week and note what sends your energy up and down or what is a neutral activity. This will be important for understanding how to maintain your energy week in and week out.

Fill out this chart with activities, groups, or even people's names who lift you up or who drain your energy. Begin to notice the subtle or not so subtle energy differences in the various activities you engage in from week to week. As you become aware, you will make better choices. This is part of being mindful. A self-care activity like getting a pedicure or going for a walk would be energy lifting. Listening to your co-worker complain for the fiftieth time about how awful their landlord is and you've tried repeatedly to help them get out of that situation would be an energy draining activity. Working on a report for work that is neither hard nor easy might be energy neutral.

ENERGY AWARENESS CHART

Energy Lifting	Energy Neutral	Energy Draining

[4]

Three Energy Modes

WHEN WE ARE SMALL children, we are told what our bodies need to live and thrive. We need to eat and drink and keep our bodies clean and get enough sleep. What is never discussed, at least overtly, is that we really need energy to get through our days as well. We never learn how to "get" energy or "maintain" energy. We know we won't have energy if we don't take care of our bodies but beyond that, we are left to our own devices. We learn when we are little how to take care of this last need on our own usually through our interactions with our parents and siblings and family members. We watch and we learn and that's just how it is.

So what many of us learn is how to "get" our energy from the people around us. I love the book, **The Celestine Prophecy** by James Redfield for all its fantastic spiritual insights written in an exciting fictional story that engages you from beginning to end. The Fourth Insight from the book is described in this way, "...we humans have always sought to increase our personal energy in the only manner we have known: by seeking to psychologically steal it from others—an unconscious competition that underlies all human conflict in the world." (Redfield, 1993) In the book, Redfield does a great job of illustrating how this works when he shows two people arguing. The character in the story actually sees the energy moving back and forth as if in a struggle between two people both trying to win the energy from the other.

This way of getting energy is detrimental to us as human beings for many reasons. First of all, it leads to increased competition and it supports the idea that there is not enough energy in the world for everyone, which is false. And this method for getting energy is not all that effective. It's unreliable because what if there is no one around to steal from? This method of getting energy stems from a disconnection from the universal energy source we discussed previously. When we feel disconnected, we can feel weak and insecure. One of the characters in Redfield's book describes it like this, "When we control another human being we receive their energy. We fill up at the other's expense and the filling up is what motivates us." (Redfield, 1993) So let's take a look at these three modes of "getting" energy to see if one of these modes is more humane, reliable, peaceful, and fun.

When you read through these three modes, you will probably see yourself somewhere in one of these modes and that is good. Please don't judge yourself or anyone else you see reflected in these modes. That's not what this is about. Remember that mindfulness is a non-judgmental state of observation. We are observing so we can consciously make a change. I have lived all of these modes and I accept that about myself. I hope you will accept it about yourself too. This is about you understanding what your current mode of "getting" energy is so you can make an overt, adult choice on what you want to do moving forward. It's also about how other people have treated us during our lives. It's important to be able to recognize what is happening on an energetic level so we know how to handle it in a heart-centered way.

These three modes of "getting" energy and moving through life are the **carp**, the **shark**, and the **dolphin**. But let's review for a second what we said about energy.

There are four types of energy but we are discussing **PERSONAL** energy here. How do you get your **PERSONAL** energy? How do you maintain it? Have you thought about this before? Where does your energy come from? What fills you up each day? If you think of your **PERSONAL** energy as a tank of gas, where is your gas station? What activities, people, situations, or environments fill you up?

Usually sleep resets our personal energy gas tank to full and we start our day there. But what happens next? How do you keep your inner gas tank continually full?

1. CARP

Living life as a carp means you get your energy almost exclusively from other people. The main way this is accomplished is by sharing stories to get attention (i.e. energy) from other people. For example, these can be the "Poor Me" stories that often display victimhood where the storyteller blames others for their problems. Some people call this the "Negative Nancy" or "Debbie Downer" type person. The main way this is accomplished is by sharing stories and demanding the other person's attention (psychologically stealing it from them and they may be entirely unaware that this is happening). These stories can range from "Poor Me" stories that often display the storyteller as the victim or they can be "Tall Tales" that are larger than life. Although these story types are different, the end goal is one and the same—your attention/energy. We'll discuss each type of storyteller so you are clear about them.

The "Poor Me" storyteller will share the negative side of any recent event that happened to them with you in full detail. And will move from one negative story to another all centered on their being the victim of the story. Or if you are already speaking, they will listen to your story about when something bad happened to you, and without responding to you or what you said, aggressively take the stage to tell his or her story about how what happened to them was even worse.

This "Poor Me" storyteller wants to "win" with the bad luck story of the year and get a "Poor you" or a hug. This is how they get attention. This is how they get their energy tank filled up. By demanding your attention, they are psychologically stealing energy from you and filling up their own tank of personal energy.

Just recently, I watched an old episode of Saturday Night Live of Debbie Downer at DisneyWorld from 2004 with guest star, Lindsey Lohan. It was a hilarious example of the carp where Rachel Dratch's character just says one negative thing after another while this Ohio family is trying to have breakfast before heading out to DisneyWorld. The cast is trying to not lose it (especially Jimmy Fallon) but by the end they can't help but outright laugh when Debbie Downer, after sharing negative news story after negative news story, finally states, "By the way, it's official. I can't have children." This is a radical stereotype of a carp but we laugh because we recognize this behavior as something we've once done or witnessed someone else do. If you haven't ever seen the skit, it is well worth finding for the laugh.

You may begin to wonder how one person can attract so many negative situations when you hear a "carp" person speak. It is because they have literally catalogued and organized all of these events in their head so they can pull a negative story quickly from their back pocket. They need to capture your attention/energy at the drop of a hat so they have to be ready always. This is how they survive and refill their personal energy gas tank so it's become important enough to know all their negative stories well and be able to recall them quickly. They keep that Rolodex of stories up to date and at the forefront of their mind. As events may happen in their lives, they may say to themselves, "Oh, this is horrible but I can't wait to tell Susan about it later."

And how do I know this? I know this because I had these same thoughts years ago when I lived mostly like a "poor me" carp. So stop that judgment going on in your mind right now. I see it. It's starting.

Or maybe you are thinking about someone who has done this to you. That is OK. Don't judge. This person just doesn't know another way YET. And if this person is you, it's OK. You're reading this book and that is a great step towards a happier life with less drama. Just reading about this will open your eyes and your awareness as to what you are doing with your words.

The "Tall Tale" storyteller will often take what you are talking about and then ramp it up and beyond. If you say you are excited that you just purchased a kayak, they will trump your story and say well, they just bought two kayaks or a small boat or even a yacht. And then they will talk non-stop about this watercraft and how cool it is. "Tall Tale" storytellers just need the attention from bettering whatever you are talking about. They may even go so far as to go buy a bigger, better kayak so they can tell you all about it. It's not that their ego is so involved; it's just that they are starving for attention (i.e. personal energy). They don't mean to be disruptive or rude. They just want to be heard and be given the energy of your attention.

I have found that sometimes these storytellers will talk non-stop if you don't try to say something or even if you do. They are fearful of gaps in the conversation because your attention may drift away from them. They will just fill the air with words sometimes just to continue to get your attention. These people may come across as disingenuous and not even realize it. The "Tall Tales" sound too big and too "tall" so the storytellers are seen as liars even though what they are saying may be quite true. It is difficult to tell as a listener whether the story is true or not. The listener feels like something is not quite right but can't put their finger on it. The storyteller is draining the listener of energy but he or she may be doing it unconsciously. The listener feels something is wrong about listening and often gets annoyed and doesn't even know why. The listener may attribute this to the storyteller being a liar when it is actually that the storyteller is psychologically stealing the listener's energy. That is what the listener feels but can't quite become consciously aware of. The listener just knows he wants to avoid this person in the future.

I call this the **Carp** way of getting personal energy. So let's get really clear on what carp do and how they do it.

Carp Characteristics

- Share negative or "tall tale" stories to get attention/energy
- Worry about the future
- Feel guilt and shame about the past
- Can often feel like the victim and blame others
- Feel powerless
- Self-judgment invades their every thought and action
- Self-centered (find it difficult to concentrate on other people's problems for long)
- View life, situations, events, or people in absolutes. Use the words "never" and "always" much of the time
- View the past as a predictor of the future
- Live from fear
- Complain or whine about many things often
- Always blame themselves first even if they are not at fault

If this sounds like you or someone you know, that's OK. I spent 30 years living as a carp so I know the mode well and have been known to slip back into it once in awhile. In the upcoming pages of this book, you will see other ways of moving through this world and just know you can choose something different for yourself than being a carp. You may find that even just becoming aware of what you have been doing to get energy begins to affect how often you become the storyteller. And as you become more aware of it, you can start to spot it quickly in the people around you.

Even though carp interact with others, they can feel lonely and isolated especially when good things happen to them. They don't know how to share the good news or talk about things in a positive way. They don't know how to make the attention last if they share a short story of good news. That doesn't give them enough of a hit or spark of personal energy. They don't allow it to or they don't know how to receive that type of attention and turn it into a source of personal energy.

Carp also may not know how to listen to others who have good news. They stand there waiting for the person to finish so they can share their next gloom and doom story. They don't comment or acknowledge the speaker or what they said. They just rush into what he or she, the carp, wants to talk about. This action leads to a lack of connection that doesn't feel good and drains some of his or her own energy. In fact, the energy of the entire group is sucked out and carp may not even be aware that this is the effect they are having. But most carp know the pain of not getting invited to the next party. This lack of connection is painful. Most positive people share stories to feel this connection but carp are not looking for that. In fact, carp may not seek out people with good news (positive people) because it makes them feel that lack of connection more sharply. Listening to positive people can also spark jealousy in the carp. This is a drain on their personal energy.

This might explain why carp often seek out other carp because they all understand each other. There is no failure at connection because that is not the point of the game although they enjoy the illusion of connection by commanding the "stage" and having other people listen. The carp game is about the person who has the best story about the worst thing that happened to him or her or the best "tall tale" and he or she wins all the energy in the room. Hanging out with other carp makes social interactions very clear and straightforward with little need for connection. Connection requires vulnerability and carp don't want to be vulnerable in any way. Positive events or having to really listen and respond to another person's story can throw them for a loop and expose vulnerabilities.

Carp don't expect other carp to really offer heartfelt responses or allow for silence and a continuation of the sharing by the other person. They don't create a healing environment for the person sharing. That is not the point. The point is to steal personal energy from others to fill up their personal gas tank.

I have been touched deeply by the work of Brené Brown and she shares a lot of great wisdom around vulnerability that is relevant here. Ms. Brown writes, "Vulnerability is the birthplace of connection and the path to the feeling of worthiness. If it doesn't feel vulnerable, the sharing is probably not constructive." (Brown, 2011) This is so succinct and incredibly stated. Only someone who has known this can write about it so well. Carp share a lot of what goes on in their lives but it is not the vulnerable share that leads to connection and worthiness. It is not constructive sharing.

Ms. Brown shares her own experience, "I spent a lot of years trying to outrun or outsmart vulnerability by making things certain and definite, black and white, good and bad. My inability to lean into the discomfort of vulnerability limited the fullness of those important experiences that are wrought with uncertainty: Love, belonging, trust, joy, and creativity to name a few." (Schawbel, 2013) This quote hit me in the heart and made me cry. I realized that this is how I had moved through the world for several years. And the lack of connection created by that mindset did indeed limit the joy and love I experienced in my life and that made me sad. I robbed myself of love. If I can help one person by sharing this one thing so no one has to rob himself or herself of love, I will feel accomplished. No one should have to go through life like this.

You see Carp avoid connection because it leads to being vulnerable which may hurt them. The carp have experienced a lot of hurt in their previous connections (usually from sharks which you will read about soon) so moving through this world in a less connected state limits how much they can get hurt. Carp convince themselves that gaining the attention of others with their story *is* love and connection but that's just an illusion. They are gaining energy but it's not the rich experience of true connection that gives our lives meaning and purpose. And one moment of true connection fills up the gas tank way faster than six hours of storytelling. If carp do successfully avoid true connection and vulnerability day after day, life can be dull and pointless. There is no depth of experience. There is no joy in simply waking to a new day. They have protected themselves so well that every day is exactly like the previous one. There are no ups and downs in their lives—no excitement, no spontaneity, no joy but they do feel safe. They will rationalize to themselves that this is a fair trade but really it just robs them of love.

A more dangerous aspect for Carp comes when they embrace this way of life with a vice-like grip. As Carp, they may come to rely **only** on negative happenings because that's all they know how to handle. It may lead to more negative things in a carp's life because that feels more comfortable to them. In fact, carp may go so far as to actively seek out negative events or allow them to happen without avoiding them. In fact, they can begin to attract more negative happenings to them because they spend so much of their time focused on them. BUT let me say that living in this carp frame of mind does NOT excuse the behaviors of anyone who hurts them or is malicious towards them. I just want to be clear on that.

So back to learning that what we focus on, we attract to us. Mike Dooley does an excellent job of teaching us this with his book, **Leveraging The Universe**, where he writes, "When you focus your thoughts (your attention) in a certain direction, you are commanding God—your thoughts—into this realm of space, it is the law that your thoughts become the things and events in your life." (Dooley, 2011) So if a carp spends all of her time contemplating the negative events of her life and labels herself a loser, do you not think that this has an effect on future events? What is she attracting with these very negative thoughts and beliefs? What is she creating when she spends all of her time cataloguing and revisiting the negative events in her past? All of her attention and focus land with the negative side of her life. When you do that, you attract more of the same. It can become an ugly cycle. That is why Dooley's motto is "Thoughts are things. Choose the good ones."

Carp are great storytellers and enjoy taking the stage (even if it's just among a few friends) to tell a good yarn and that can be a very positive thing. Storytelling is very important in our society and can be a great way to share knowledge and increase connection. The thing to keep in mind with storytelling is why the story is being told. Is the purpose of the story to increase sharing and connection or to steal energy from the listener? That makes all the difference.

Internal thoughts of the Carp:

- I don't deserve... [insert anything from a new job that pays well to happiness to romance]
- I'm not good enough. I never have been and I never will be.
- I don't know how other people are happy. I don't get it.
- I worry all the time that I'll lose my job, my romantic partner, my house, my car, etc.
- I am not a very good person.
- I feel like my life is out of control.
- Everyone always ruins everything for me.
- No one will ever love me.
- I feel like no one really cares about what happens to me.
- I feel like no one really listens to me.
- I will never get over that time that [insert situation or person or event here] happened to me. I guess I deserved that.
- I'll never have anything good because last time I did, I lost it and that really hurt. I don't want to go through that again.
- That [one event] is going to ruin the rest of my life.

- I am [insert adjective here --overweight, insecure, lack confidence, ugly, socially awkward] because of [insert name here or event here]. I'll never change. I'll always be this way.

This is called negative self-talk and it brings your energy down even more. It can send you into spirals of anxiety and depression. It's important to listen to the storytelling you do in your own head. What soundtrack do you have going? What station are you listening to? We'll circle back to this later.

A great teacher of mine, Beatrex Quntanna, who I love and admire, once, asked me an interesting question in her astrology and tarot class. She asked us "When you tell someone your story, what is the date of the event you start with?" What is the burning story you must share with this new person you've just met? It may not even relate to what you are talking about but you feel this strong desire to share this story. Look at this story and when it took place in your life. Is it a positive story? Or are you trying to gain sympathy and attention from this new person by telling it? Be honest. This is important because it will show you where you are stuck. Basically, you are living from that moment in time and you are not living in the present. Carp do not live in the present moment. They are stuck in an event in the pFor example, when I used to meet people and I was in Carp mode, I would always bring up the fact that my husband battled cancer when my son was just three months old. That event was tragic for me so I was stuck in it. I wanted them to know that my life had been terrible at that point. I wanted them to know that so badly about me. I wanted to see their eyes look away and compassion and attention be poured over me. I needed it—that energy and attention. It was an effective "Poor Me" story that worked for many, many years. I think my son was 8 years old when Beatrex asked me what story I was stuck in and I had a very extreme "A-ha" moment as I realized I was rooted back there in that terrible situation. Telling that story over and over again kept me stuck back there. I couldn't move forward. So, I made a conscious effort from that moment on to move forward and not let that one event define who I was in THE PRESENT MOMENT.

That event was a very real part of me but the helplessness and the sense of being a victim did not have to travel with me at the forefront of my mind anymore. The victimhood I felt did not have to define who I was. I didn't want it to be my constant travel companion. I wanted a new definition of who I was in THIS moment. I didn't want to carry these many bags of sadness, terror, and loneliness with me now. (My husband survived two surgeries and radiation treatment and has been cancer free since then. Thank goodness.) But let me say this, it is only when we repeatedly tell a story over and over for the distinct goal of getting attention that the storytelling becomes an unhealthy practice.

When my husband was first diagnosed with cancer, I was so overcome with sadness and fear that I couldn't even share the story with others at that time. It was so terrible that I couldn't even get it out to get attention. Instead I clammed up and shared nothing with anyone. That was not helpful either. I couldn't work through any of it by hiding it away or standing in denial.

So I want you to know that I do believe, and hear me on this, that sharing what happens in our lives, especially tragic, sad, and messed up things, is critically important. That is part of the healing process and helps us understand what has happened to us or at least to lessen the emotions around the event. By not talking about it, we do ourselves a disservice. I finally opened up about it a few months after it happened and shared with a few people and got a few appointments with a therapist, which I found very helpful. I could share and cry and show anger and all of these different emotions that were like storms flowing through me. After about a year or so, I began to seek out instances where I could tell people I knew about what happened to me. And there comes a point where it moves from

Three Energy Modes | 55

the sharing being a helpful, healing thing to do and into a need to get someone's attention/energy.

Here is an example to illustrate the difference. Let's say you speak to someone and ask them why they look sad or are crying and that person gives you a very detailed description of how they lost their pet and how much it is upsetting to them. You give them a hug and tell them how sorry you are for their loss. You are curious and are making conversation so you inquire as to when this happened. Then you are shocked to hear that this event took place over 20 years ago. Smack!

That's when you know someone has been telling that story for far too long and only tells it to get attention. The telling of that story has gone from a part of the healing process to a "poor me" call for attention and energy. Do you get the difference? And beyond that, this person is stuck back there in that story and has consciously chosen to not move into the present moment and that's sad. The person is missing all of the beauty of life that is happening now.

2. The Shark

Living as a shark is similar to the carp in that sharks get their energy almost exclusively from other people too. Sharks use shame, guilt, fear, intimidation, gossip, and anger to pull energy from other people. These people often manipulate others so they can take their energy. Again, this is a means of survival often learned as a child and it may only appear when the shark feels threatened or is low on energy. Or the shark has learned this behavior from others in his or her family and it's all he or she knows how to be in the world. Again, by beginning to become aware of this behavior, we can clearly choose something else and make it a conscious choice.

I had a really interesting experience in the spring and summer of 2010. I had worked at a particular job for five years but in the last 12 months of this job, I was not getting along with my boss. Her behavior towards me changed and she became what I call "shark-like" playing manipulative games and bullying me. She was very passive-aggressive saying that I was doing great work to my face and smiling at me but then turning around and not reviewing my work. She would not even attend our team meetings where I was to present my work for her review and approval.

One particular morning, I had arranged a team meeting with her and four other people to review a report I wrote about the findings of a survey. We needed to discuss the survey to make some decisions about what to do going forward in the whole department. My boss said she would be there but then did not show up. Time passed and we sat around waiting. We decided it was pointless to start without her so we all just worked on our laptops until she came. She didn't show up for an hour and a half and was then upset with me and the other team members for not starting without her. This is typical shark-like behavior. She stole my energy and the energy of my teammates all morning long even before she got there. That's one of the tricky things about sharks. They don't have to be in the same room with you to steal your energy. It can be a long distance thing and they know this.

I was tired of being the victim of her shark games (and I didn't like who I was becoming in that situation) so I left for a new part-time position at a defense company. After two months of working there (which I did not enjoy), I was asked to come to the Vice-President's office along with my supervisor. I was puzzled but entered the office and sat down. The Vice-President quite pointedly accused me of taking more than my regular pay by accepting paychecks that were accidentally billed out as full-time instead of part-time. He asked me to write a check for the amount I'd been overpaid right then and there. My supervisor looked on neither supporting me nor accusing me. I was flabbergasted and told them I had no idea I'd been paid more than I deserved. It was so hard to tell on those checks just exactly what I was getting paid by the time they take out taxes and everything. I told them that I had turned in the correct timesheets each week with my under 20 hours a week on them. The Vice-President looked me over and made me squirm (much like a shark would) waiting to see if he wanted to take another bite out of me or let me loose. He decided I was telling the truth and told me to collect my personal items and to leave the building immediately. And his final parting shot was informing me that I would not be receiving my final paycheck. Whoa. I couldn't believe it. I went from one shark to another in a matter of weeks. What was going on?

 I decided to work for my church for a little while. They offered me a small monthly stipend to work part-time on their social media. I thought this would be a safe gig while I figured out what was next. I thought things were going well but I had questioned the way my manager was doing things and how she was spending church money. Oh boy. Another shark reared its ugly head and took me to the conference room for an "evaluation" which turned into an all out verbal attack on me. Whoa. Really? Again?

 I took some time off then and I gathered my wits about me and tried to analyze what I had been creating. Obviously, something was going on because I'd come into contact with the same kind of person three times in a row within just a few months. I've heard that when the same type of people keep coming into your life, you are just not getting the lesson they are bringing you. So, I thought about it and tried to analyze it but I don't think I got too far until much later.

 So, what do you think was happening in these three situations? What was I supposed to learn? Is there any direct connection between the carp and the shark? Does it take one of each to really create drama in our lives? Was I being a carp? Was I being the victim? Was that just too enticing for three sharks in a row? Was I setting myself up for each one of these situations? What could I have done differently? Do you think it was a coincidence that I ran into another shark after leaving the first one and then the second one? I don't. I think after I left that first job, I felt very much like a victim and I carried that residue with me into the next two situations. Sharks need carp for their victims (to steal energy from) and carp need sharks to be the villain in the stories that they tell to get energy. There is a symbiosis here. They need each other. One does not exist without the other.

Recognizing my own part in creating those situations was a huge realization for me. I might just be understanding it in full as a result of writing this book. I was given the perfect situations to write about and illustrate this point for you. I don't want you to have to go through life either as a shark or as a carp. Both are unsatisfying and can be painful. That was a painful summer for me and I think it is still affecting me on some level. I'll tell you that I'm not real keen to work in an office again.

I will admit that I got a lot of mileage out of these stories as a carp for a while. Three hits in a row made for a powerful carp story especially the part about being accused of knowingly accepting paychecks that were too big and being told to leave the building immediately like I was some sort of criminal. You see how that works, right? I needed the sharks to give me the incredible "poor me" stories that I could share to get sympathy and attention.

James Redfield does a great job of describing sharks in **The Celestine Prophecy** when one of his characters says "All this is still unconscious in most people. All we know is that we feel weak and when we control others we feel better. What we don't realize is that this sense of feeling better costs the other person. It is their energy we have stolen. Most people go through their lives in a constant hunt for someone else's energy." (Redfield, 1993) Does this sound like a shark to you? Have we all met someone like this before?

There are many different kinds of sharks in the world and I probably can't even list them all here. Some shark-like behaviors can include backhanded compliments, smiling while delivering a dagger-like piece of criticism, passive-aggressive behavior, using fear or blackmail to manipulate you into doing something you don't want to do, yelling, "the silent treatment," or making big scenes in public places or in front of others whom you want to respect and trust you.

Sharks will make you feel like a fool, embarrass you, or spread gossip about you. Their only goal is to get you to comply any way they can while simultaneously making sure they still look good. And in so doing, they win and steal your energy. You don't even have to be in the room for them to steal your energy. Sharks use these means to take you down so they look better because their confidence is actually very shaky and fragile. This is the only way they know how to get energy and keep moving forward. This is their way of staying in control and they are afraid their world will fall apart if they let go of this way of doing things.

One type of shark is the fake **Mr. Nice Guy Shark** who smiles and says to take as much as you want but then mutters under their breath that you shouldn't have any because you look like a whale. Or the shark that just doesn't give you boundaries for how much to take from them and then you take thinking that it's OK. But in the next minute, that same shark begins to avoid and/or resent you because you took so much. There is also the **Make You Feel Guilty Shark** where she uses guilt to manipulate you into visiting her at work or picking up her kids from school or whatever you don't really want to do but feel like you should. Have you ever come across someone like that?

A shark can be the **Ms. Office Gossip Shark**. I've known lots of different versions of this type of person and generally try to stay away. This person has the dirt on everyone everywhere and knows exactly (or at least thinks they know) what everyone else is doing and why. They enjoy being the center of attention with the latest bit of gossip so they can grab your attention/energy and at the same time, think they are making themselves look better than whomever they are gossiping about. Their ego thinks they are making themselves look good and the dishing out on others gives them a desperate jolt of energy that keeps them going. There is also the **EPIC Shark**, which bites you and takes you down without any provocation—just because he or she can. It's good to know they are out there too.

Sharks can be the loud, aggressive manager who barks orders and loves to watch you beg for a change in the shift schedule. They enjoy their power so much they laud it over you and can't wait for instances to manipulate and embarrass you so they can look bigger and better. Sharks can be the parent at the baseball game who criticizes not only the coach for every move he makes (loudly from the stands) while also criticizing his own boy in front of everyone. Sharks can be quiet and behind the scenes digging up secrets to use against you to get you to do their bidding. Sharks are the bullies on the playground who take your lunch money and hit you on the arm just because they can.

Sharks are a tricky sort but we must remember that they learned this behavior, as a means of surviving so please don't judge. And remember most of us have probably tried on the shark mask ourselves at least once or twice and that is OK. Sometimes we may need to in order to defend ourselves in certain situations. That is needed sometimes. So, please try to enter into this with eyes wide open and acceptance of yourself and others just as they are. We are all doing the best we can in this moment with the experiences we have had so far in our lives. This is a learned behavior that can be changed to a more heart-centered way of being in the world.

Let's look at the characteristics of the shark for more clarity.

Shark Characteristics

- Use shame, guilt, fear, intimidation, manipulation, and anger to pull energy out of others.
- Always looking for next victim who is full of energy (not focused on present - future focused)
- Lives in the past as they feel it is a predictor of the future

- Need to feel in control ALWAYS and in every respect
- Ego-centered—concerned about image and looking good, narcissistic
- Very reactive and sensitive to criticism but covers that up with anger
- Judgmental of others
- All or nothing thinking (e.g. kill or be killed), everything is all good or all bad
- Isolated from others emotionally, never had a safe place to share feelings
- •Lives from fear, motivated by fear
- Always blame others first even if they know they are at fault

Sharks are highly sensitive and are always watching others for signs of weakness so they can prey upon them and steal their energy. Just like sharks in the wild smell the first drop of blood, so do people who move through this world as sharks. They are very observant and watch every action by others to see if they can gather evidence or ammunition to use against that person at a later date.

Sharks think 3 or 4 moves ahead of others and consider themselves quite smart and above others but they often end up feeling isolated and lonely as a result of these behaviors. They are quite sensitive and just want to be loved and feel a connection with others but often can't figure out how to make that happen authentically. They judge others but they also judge themselves even more harshly. They never feel good enough or worthy of whatever position they find themselves in or whatever good they cobble together for themselves although they will never let you know this. They feel like it all may get taken away from them at any moment. They live in fear of that.

The sharks know that their intimidating behavior is not really what makes a good human being but they try to tell themselves a story about why they have to be this way in the world and they stick to that. They hold tight to that story as it gives them comfort when they are feeling lonely.

If you are having trouble picturing a shark, think of Darth Vader or Emperor Palpatine from **Star Wars** or what about Scarecrow from **Batman** or Lex Luthor from **Superman**. Most villains are sharks ruling by fear and intimidation. Think of your favorite movie or book and imagine the villain. He or she is most probably a shark.

BUT remember that shark behavior falls on a sliding scale and that your next-door neighbor who yells and manipulates you is no Darth Vader. Each of us has embraced the shark mask even if it was just for a short period of time. Be accepting. Don't judge. We each learned these skills as a means of survival but it also means we can learn a new and better way.

See if the following thoughts ring a bell and help you think through what is feels like to be a shark.

Internal Thoughts of the Shark:
- If I don't take control, no one will.
- I strike first so I never get hurt.
- I leave first so I never get hurt.
- Everyone is so… [insert adjective here like stupid, ignorant, lame, etc.].
- I feel lonely and so above everyone else.
- I don't always feel good about what I do to others but I don't see how else to get ahead in this world.
- Sometimes it feels so good to just take someone down and make them cry.
- It's just too easy sometimes to bend people and make them do what I want.
- I always get my way.
- Power is a drug I can't resist.
- I am always in control. I never let my guard down because that's when you get into trouble.

- Most people are weak and pathetic. It's sad, really, how naive they are.
- Never show your weakness.
- It's a dog eat dog world.
- People need to toughen up or get out of my sight.
- I can take anything I want in this world.
- The only way I can get what I want in this life is by force (through guilt, manipulation, fear, anger, etc.).
- No one shares or gives stuff away for free. There's always a catch. There is no free lunch.
- It's my way or the highway.

Sharks become sharks because they learned how to do it from a family member who was an even bigger, meaner shark. Or they lived with carp and it was easier to just get the energy they wanted by being a shark. Or sometimes we're sharks with certain people and carp when we're with other people. It may just depend on who we are with. Sharks may evoke carp-like qualities within us sometimes and we may look in the mirror and not recognize ourselves when this happens. Or carp may evoke shark-like qualities in you. You may want to review situations that make you feel less than your normal self. Who are you with? How do they treat you? How do you react? Does being with them get your back up like you are up against the wall? There is probably a shark in the waters and you will need to decide what to do in that case. Read on for some wisdom and clarity on what to do.

3. THE SHARK AND THE CARP AS MASKS

I'll let you in on a secret now that you know more about the shark and the carp. We are not born as sharks or carp. The good news is we are all born as dolphins. Yay! We are all dolphins underneath it all (you'll read more about them in a few pages and see that this is a really good thing). We learn early to adopt the masks of the carp and the shark to just muddle through. That is all these are—just masks that we can take on and off. I know because not only did I have a well-worn carp mask but I also occasionally wore the shark mask (and although I am reluctant to admit this, I still get both of these masks out once in awhile). Sometimes I really needed to and I accept that about myself just as I ask you to accept this in yourself and in others you meet. Understanding about the masks gives you the means to consciously choose something else—a better way to be in this woThe time I can recall being a shark most clearly was with my son when he was little. He would be so full of energy and vibrant and happy and I would feel listless, tired, and exhausted. I was not taking care of myself and some days it was just too much and I'd yell at my son (this was your normal yelling—nothing vicious and yet I feel bad about it even now). I'd get angry with him over something so not worth getting angry over. And you know what happened? I stole my son's energy every time I yelled at him. Afterwards, I'd feel a bit better energetically because I got a boost from him but at the same time, on an unconscious level, I knew that this was not the kind of mother I wanted to be. I knew I was doing something wrong and yet, I saw other moms and dads do this. It was normal, right? But this thought did nothing to elevate my energy level so I'd be back to where I was before feeling tired and exhausted and then add to that, feeling like a failure as a mom. Acting like a shark did nothing to improve my situation.

I know I didn't want to parent like this but I couldn't find a way out when I was feeling so low. Thinking back on my fits of yelling at my son brings tears to my eyes now. I now know there is a better way to be but maybe it was going through that during my son's younger years that helped me get to this realization and be a better parent now. And for that, I'm thankful. And I better understand when I see other parents doing their best with their kids. I know. I was there in their shoes. And I am still there.

My son is a teenager now and I am so glad I began to understand more about energy several years ago. Yes, I'm thankful now but so not perfect either. And I really want you to get this about the sharks and the carp because it affects all of our relationships—not just at work but the relationships with those we love the most. And it can do terrible damage. Stealing our children's energy creates the need for a defense mechanism. This means that our kids as a result, learn to wear the masks of sharks and carp to defend themselves. Do you see how that cycle continues from parents to child to that child's kids and so on? A lot of damage can be passed down from one generation to another this way. How much are we still hurting from those times that our parents or siblings stole our energy by wearing the shark or carp mask when we were little? I know it still hurts me. Let's make a change, shall we?

PLEASE NOTE! BIG RED ARROW POINTING DOWN FOR PARENTS!

This is one of the main reasons I am writing this book. I want to share this with you and have you understand how to be a more energy aware parent who does not need to steal energy from your kids. The energy aware parent learns how to boost their child's energy and instructs them on how to get and maintain their own energy. Understanding the importance of energy in our relationships is a game changer for parents and children. If there's one thing you can do for your kids that makes a huge difference, it's being responsible for your own energy creation and maintenance and being an example to them on how to do this. And that brings us to learning about the dolphin.

4. THE DOLPHIN

The good news is that underneath it all, we are all dolphins. Yay! We were born dolphins but sometimes we have needed to don a mask. These were the masks of the carp and the shark. And sometimes we still need those masks occasionally to get through a tough time. BUT underneath that mask lies a dolphin waiting to be free and to live life more fully and happily.

Every dolphin gets his or her energy from the universal source of energy. Dolphins do not get their energy from other people. They connect on a deep level to all that is or to the universe or to God/Goddess or the Force or whatever you want to call it. This gives dolphins an advantage over carp and sharks because they don't need other people to fill up their gas tank. They can fill up anywhere at any time. In the book, **The Celestine Prophecy**, James Redfield's character describes the Fourth Insight and shares that as people begin to understand this struggle for energy that "We would begin to break free from the competition over mere human energy because we would finally be able to receive our energy from another source." (Redfield, 1993) Dolphins understand this and know how to connect and fill up their gas tank from the source of universal energy.

There are many methods of connection and different people have different things that work for them. Some ways to do this might be a breathing practice, meditation, prayer, singing, dancing, positive affirmations, making music, painting, spending time with animals, exercise, creative ventures, just being in nature, or any combination thereof. I do find that meditation works best and most mindfulness books will lead you in this direction because it is effective. But I am hesitant to restrict it just to meditation. I want to encourage everyone to find their own way to connect and fill up.

Everyone can feel it when an individual practices deep connection because it creates a lightness in their energy field that people notice. Carp feel safe because the dolphin will not steal their energy and sharks feel less like a bully because there is no need to take energy. Dolphins, by being who they are, emit energy to those they come in contact with. This sets everyone at ease and brings about peaceful relations. Even if there is only one dolphin in the room, their energy brings calmness to those around him or her.

Some side effects of living more like a dolphin (which I practice as much as possible but am still working at) are a steady increase in happiness, contentment, loving feelings towards one's self and others, and healthier, more fulfilling relationships. You may notice that the more you live like a dolphin, you may not feel like hanging out with all the same people you used to hang out with and that is OK. It's a sign that you are transforming and you will begin to attract more dolphins to you. So you may see new friends show up. You also may find yourself stopping in mid-conversation becoming aware of what you are saying and why—noticing shark or carp behavior. And that's good. Your awareness is increasing.

These are all good signs. I remember when I was trying to leave my carp mask behind more often, I sometimes found it hard to find topics of conversation. I'd think through what I was going to say and reject every topic because they were just me complaining or whining so I'd just be quiet. That is a good sign too. You will find with time that silence and listening is quite nice and that when you speak, you have thoughtful, positive things to say. People will lean in to hear what you have to say because they recognize that you are thoughtful about what you choose to put out into the world. And that's nice.

Feeling more resilient and stronger during life's tough moments is common to all dolphins. It's difficult to live 100% of the time as a dolphin. It does, however, become a healthy habit more and more often leading to deeper satisfaction and peace. For me personally, I notice that similar to a dolphin, my life flows with grace and ease way more now as a result of living this way. I get to spend more moments in bliss and joy and for that, alone, I am so grateful.

So what does it mean to live like a dolphin? Let's look at these characteristics.

Dolphin Characteristics

- Get their energy from a universal source (not from other people)
- Live in the present (mindful)
- Feel empowered, value-minded, and aware of who they are
- Non-judgmental, accepting of others
- Focus on what they want more of in their life to attract it to them, use their attention wisely
- Go with the flow
- Have clearly defined boundaries of how they want others to treat them, how they want to spend their time, and who they want to spend it with
- Have learned to say No gracefully (No is a complete sentence)
- Deep compassion for others
- Live their lives from a space of love, not fear
- Accept their imperfections in themselves and others
- Are responsible for their own energy
- Have learned to trust their inner voice
- Regulate self-talk
- Accept that life is neither black nor white but consists of lots of gray—rejects the polarity of words like "never" or "always"
- Live in an open manner with no secrets
- Trusts the universe is unfolding as it should for their best and highest good
- Trusts that there is always enough of everything for everyone so greed is pointless
- Understand that they don't know everything—child's point of view looking to learn something new every day, recognizing that each person has something to teach them

- Know the power of words and thoughts in creating their life
- Joy and playfulness are the best way to "work" or "get things done"
- Listen to signs from the universe and follow the flow

Carp and sharks believe that life is a constant struggle over what is perceived as a limited supply of personal energy. They believe they are at war with everyone they meet over this energy. But dolphins know that there is a limitless supply of universal energy meaning there is plenty to go around. This awareness leads to peaceful, positive relations. With dolphins, there are no power plays, no displays of ego, and no greed. There is no point to that kind of behavior. Being the dolphin allows for play and flow and purposeful activities to move forward that work for the benefit of all.

Dolphins learn how to get their energy each day whether that's with a brisk walk in nature, a ten-minute meditation, or writing in a gratitude journal to set themselves up positively for the day. They know what works for them to get what I call "heart-centered." This is a state of compassion for oneself and for the entire world where love is the bottom line every time. There is no judgment, only acceptance. There is only the love in the present moment for all that is, exactly as it is. It really doesn't matter how you get heart-centered as long as you do it consistently and every day. It's a good goal to try to remain heart-centered for as much of your day as possible.

I find that for me, meditation works well but I also need to move my body in some way or another and it helps if that movement is in nature (like taking a walk around the neighborhood or along the ocean). Some days, a walk on the beach does it for me and sometimes thinking about ten things I'm grateful for can do it.

The real key to the practice is to become aware throughout your day of your energy and maintain it just like you do your own hunger or thirst. When you are hungry or thirsty, you become aware of a growling in your stomach or a dry mouth and you take action to care for your body. To stay in a state of flow like the dolphin, you must tend to your energy level in the same way and stay aware of how high or low it is and take action to regulate it. It's a constant practice but well worth it. And it becomes very clear when you have neglected to take care of your energy level because that's when things stop flowing, communication with loved ones becomes strained or angry, and you tense up. As far as I can tell, life is too short to spend much time in that kind of state. I prefer the love, flow, and playfulness afforded the dolphin.

I remember when I was first married that I could stay angry for days at a time over something my husband did. I chose to stay angry and give him the "silent treatment." I've now got that down to hours and sometimes, just minutes of being angry. I try to identify the reason why I am angry sooner and take responsibility for my part of that. And if there is something to discuss with my husband, I do it sooner than later and make sure I come from a place of heart-centeredness and true wonder at how to resolve the matter. Then we can create a safe space for a heartfelt conversation where I can share my feelings and my boundaries about how I want to be treated and he can share what he needs or wants. The problem can get resolved quickly and no one (hardly ever) goes to bed mad in our house. This choice to be the dolphin helps this happen and you can choose it too. Life is much too short to spend so much time being angry or upset. I like to have things resolved and back into a space of love as soon as possible in our house.

Internal thoughts of the Dolphin:

- I'm not perfect and that's OK.
- I love and accept myself as I am in this moment.
- I am heart-centered and make decisions from a space of love.

- I try to breathe and get heart-centered before having difficult conversations with my loved ones.
- When something jars me emotionally, my first response is to breathe and reflect before I respond.
- I try to monitor my energy level throughout the day.
- I plan activities during the day to get heart-centered, take care of myself, and keep my energy up.
- I take good care of myself so that I can take care of others.
- I am dedicated to self-care.
- I try to make good food choices, exercise often, and get a good amount of sleep.
- I dedicate myself to living love every day.
- I am a masterpiece AND a work in progress.
- I make a point to be grateful every day.
- I find beauty wherever I am and appreciate it.
- I strive to see the best in people.
- I recognize that just as I am doing my best so is everyone else.
- I am generous with my love, attitude, and kind words.
- I strive to offer compliments over criticism.
- I try to be a force for love in the world spreading it around wherever I go.
- I am responsible for the energy I bring to everyone and every situation.
- If my energy is off, I stop and fix it immediately.
- People are a real kick and I enjoy spending time with all types of people. There is always something I can learn from them.
- I look forward to a new adventure every day in life. You never know what will come your way.
- I focus on what I want to create more of in my life.

If you are unclear as to what it looks like to be a dolphin in this world, spend some time with kids under the age of 8. They know how it goes. They expect happiness, fun, and to be completely cared for by the universe (and their parents) each day. They greet each day as an adventure and another opportunity to be with the ones they love and to have fun together. Life is ice cream cones, running through the grass, digging in the dirt, and trips to the playground with family and friends.

Kids love life. They see the beauty around them by just playing with the dandelions in the backyard or making mud pies. Everything is play. Be more like kids. Play, laugh, and enjoy your loved ones, soak up the sun on your face, and feel the grass between your toes. Kids enjoy the heck out of every moment. They don't spend much time thinking about yesterday or worrying about tomorrow. They are very good at that. Sometimes I think our kids are here to remind us to live in the moment. We worry so much as parents and don't always enjoy each moment.

Sometimes the spirit of the universe has a sense of humor and reminds you of this. My son was about five years old and loved to play at the playground at the park near our house. Usually, he wanted me to play with him and play monster by chasing him around the playground or throw a big ball back and forth. On this day, my energy was low. I was tired and cranky and was not taking very good care of myself. I just wanted to sit on the bench and not do anything. My son wanted me to play, of course, but I put him off and told him to go down the slide or just do something.

Meanwhile, there were a few kids playing with a big rubber ball behind me near the bench I was sitting on and occasionally that ball would get kicked near me. As my mind flew into disarray, thinking about how badly my day had gone and worrying about how the rest of the day would go, I became less and less energetic. I was running a particularly harsh script in my head about how I wasn't doing a good job as a mom and was so tired and what was I going to do about naptime, etc. Would he go to sleep? Would I get to rest? Blah, blah, blah....

Next thing I know my brain registered a blow to the back of my head from that big rubber ball. It didn't really hurt—just startled me. And I had to chuckle because it seemed like a nudge from the universe to get up off my butt and go play. It was a real kick in the pants to get away from thoughts that were draining my energy and go be in the present moment on the playground with my son. So I did. I got up off that bench and began playing monster with my son. My energy, instead of draining more, got pumped up because I was having fun. Before I knew it, I was laughing and hugging my son. I silently thanked the universe for literally hitting me upside the head to go play. Dolphins listen to signs from the universe and follow the flow. This was a good example of that.

A Review

Let's review the differences between the carp, the shark, and the dolphin.

Type	Characteristics	Internal Thoughts
Carp	-Tells "Poor Me" or "Tall Tale" stories for attention/energy, needs a bad guy -Always looking for next person to tell their story to so they can get energy -Worry about the future -Feels like the victim, powerless -Lives from fear -Self-centered, judges self harshly, blames self often	"I'm not good enough." "I don't deserve…." "I worry all the time that I will lose…." "No one will ever love me." "No one cares what happens to me." "It's hopeless. I'll always be this way."
Shark	-Uses shame, guilt, fear, intimidation, manipulation, and anger to pull energy from others, -Always looking for next victim to get energy from -Lives in the past and feels it is a predictor of the future always -Needs to feel in control always and in every respect -Ego-centered, narcissistic -Lives from fear -Blames others for everything	"I strike first so I never get hurt." "It's too easy to bend people and make them do what I want." "I always get my way." "Power is a drug I can't resist." "Most people are weak and pathetic. It's sad, really, how naïve they are." "It's a dog eat dog world." "I can take anything I want in this world." "It's my way or the highway."

Dolphin	-Get their energy from a universal source (not other people) -Live in the present, mindful -Feel empowered, value-minded, and aware of who they are -Non-judgmental, accepting of others -Lives from love -Lives in the flow but with boundaries -Trusts in the universe is unfolding as it should	"I love and accept myself and others." "I breathe and reflect when something jars me emotionally and then I respond." "I try to monitor my energy level throughout the day." "I am dedicated to taking good care of myself." "I look for beauty and practice gratitude." "I put my attention on what I want to attract more of into my life."

5. A Carp, A Shark, and a Dolphin Walk Into A Bar...

We live in a world full of carp, sharks, and dolphins so what's a person to do? If you have tried to observe the people around you and have begun to recognize the different energy types, you may find yourself surrounded by a school of carp or even several sharks. What's a dolphin to do?

I know there are a lot of women who get together for happy hour at a bar and just have a carp fest. Sometimes they whine, complain, and blame but sometimes they don't. You can make a difference in a group like this if you want to create a more dolphin-like atmosphere. It just takes one person to steer a ship and it can be you if you feel like stepping into that role.

If one person needs to air out a situation then let them do that. But if it's the same old story you've all heard a hundred times, then maybe its time to redirect that conversation. Focus everyone on the positive. Focus everyone on what they can be grateful for or how good the food is or how nice the weather has been. Change it up.

Tell a story of how something good happened to you or to a friend of yours. This can be enough to shake up the carp energy and replace it with something more positive.

If your friends see you leaving your carp mask behind, they might be more likely to drop theirs as well. What you will usually find is that there is more than one dolphin in the group but that dolphin is not quite sure what to do to change the tide. If you start in with a positive focus, usually the first person to support the new topic of conversation is a dolphin just waiting for the opportunity to help shift the conversation. Use this to your advantage.

6. Tools for the Carp Party

Whether you are encountering just one carp or a whole happy hour crew, here are some tips so you can stay in dolphin mode.

A. Be mindful.
B. Redirect the conversation.
C. Bring energy to the group.
D. Use energy shifters.
E. If you have to carp, keep it short.
F. Take care of yourself.

A. Be mindful.

Recognize the mode of conversation. What are people saying? How are they saying it? Do you feel like someone wants your energy or is starting to grab it? Is this carp-like behavior you are experiencing or is this a shark? Don't fall into it. Don't start saying "I'm sorry" and listening intently to the "poor me" story or whatever the carp is saying. Detach a bit and observe. Take stock of your energy level and be aware if the energy should dip. Then remember the strategies listed below for how to handle the situation.

B. Redirect the conversation.

Think of a positive and uplifting story or TV program or movie you saw that you could talk about in this group. Plan ahead and think of possible topics to bring up like vacations or the best movie they have ever seen or book recommendations. Make sure to watch yourself during the get together to notice if you begin to want to shift into carp mode to get a story in. Stop yourself. And then think of another personal experience that is positive and uplifting. Or find a way to share that story and not end it with people saying they're sorry for you. Find a happy ending or way of viewing the situation that is uplifting or interesting. Or can you think of a feel good story you want to share about your life or about someone else you read about? Sharing this type of story will do much for your energy and the energy of the group. Having a change of topic ready to go can also be helpful if the group gets too carp-y all of a sudden. Remember when you say "I'm sorry," to someone who is giving you a "poor me" story, you are giving them permission to continue and you are giving them your energy and attention. So take control and redirect the conversation in a more positive direction.

C. Bring energy to the group.

Get in your heart-centered energy mode before you even meet up with anyone so you can bring good energy to the social situation. Get yourself big and full of lots of energy. Sing and dance and pump yourself up before you even enter a room with one or more carp. This can do a lot in terms of shifting the energy. Seriously, it can. One person can truly make a difference. If carp see one person not wearing the usual mask, others may choose not to wear theirs. Being a dolphin can really catch on and be contagious. But you have to watch it and keep your energy high. Remember to breathe and look for ways to keep your energy up while you are there.

D. Use energy shifters.

Energy shifters are specific things you can do in a conversation to just shake things up from the usual pitter-patter of carp conversations. With a break like this, the energy shifts and you can redirect it. Humor is a great energy shifter. Do you have something funny you can share? Humor is great for breaking up carp conversations. It relieves the tension and allows more freedom in the range of topics. And usually when someone shares a funny story, someone else has one too. It keeps the conversation light and brings energy to the group. Laughing is always a good thing as long as it is not at someone else's expense. These should not be gossip stories but good stories about truly funny things that happened where no one was hurt or embarrassed (unless you are the embarrassed one in the story which is OK and even encouraged). Sharing stories of your own bumbling or mistakes can be great fun and give you lots of energy as others find your experience funny and it gives them a boost.

Another energy shifting technique is to pay the carp a compliment. This usually throws them off and they may actually not even know what to say. Then that's good. You have given them attention and energy but you were in control of how much and for how long. After paying the compliment, it might be a good time to change topics or excuse yourself and get out of there.

Unexpected questions asked of a carp can also clip the unending storytelling. The carp is surprised and caught off guard, as you are not participating as other carp do. It may muddy their storyline or give you enough of a pause to introduce a new topic or walk away after they answer.

E. If you have to carp, keep it short.

It might be difficult to leave all carp behavior behind for an entire group of friends so this idea might make a nice compromise. I know one woman who often gets together with three friends and they have a pact. They can complain and whine for the first ten minutes of their time together and then that's it. They have to stop and they will call each other on it if they get off track again. This is a proactive and great way to handle it when not all members are ready to be dolphins 100% of the time. Being open about the need to occasionally complain but not let it rule the conversation and bring everyone down is a very dolphin thing to do.

F. *Take care of you.*

Sometimes you cannot always turn the tide of the group and it may go ALL OUT CARP. You may feel your energy draining away. You may try to change the topic or tell a funny story, but it all falls on deaf ears and the biggest carp continues with their poor me story or whatever it is that day. If you feel your energy draining and that this situation is no longer supporting you in being a dolphin, you can take care of yourself. You can excuse yourself to the bathroom to just get your bearings, take a few breaths, and evaluate the situation. Will the situation get better? Can you get yourself heart-centered again?

An effective tool for taking care of you is visualizing an impenetrable white bubble of light and energy around yourself. This protects you from anyone trying to take your energy away, whether they are consciously doing it or not. Remember carp steal your energy by telling stories. It's up to you if you want to give all your energy away. If you choose to take care of yourself, you can prevent this from happening. If you don't feel the situation is going to get better and that you predict your energy will be completely gone if you stay with this group, politely excuse yourself and leave. That is always an option.

Another technique for re-centering yourself in love is to practice gratitude. Think of at least ten things that you are grateful for right then. Really feel into each item on your list and it can get you back to being a dolphin.

If you always travel together with someone to these events, then make sure you have another way to get home on your own so you can leave at any time. This is not mean or awful to your friends. This is you taking care of yourself. There is no need to justify this to anyone. If your friends don't understand then you might want to re-evaluate just what these friendships are bringing to your life. Friends should want what is best for you in each and every moment. They should want you to take care of yourself when you need to. If you don't have any dolphin friends, then maybe it's time to look around a bit and expand your network. There are dolphins out there looking for a friend like you too.

7. Tools for a Shark Encounter

There are some similarities between how to handle carp and sharks and you'll see that shortly. Sharks tend to be a bit more isolated and less prone to be in large groups but these tips really work for one on one or in groups.

First of all, breathe. Don't take anything this shark has to say personally. Dolphins use a pause button and do not feel the need to react right away. Think about what is said. Take it in. Pause. Reflect. Then maintain your cool and respond. Know who you are. Know what your values are. Protect your energy field. Breathe. When the shark feels like you are not going to give up your energy, two things can happen. The shark may intensify his or her efforts to get energy from you or they may give up and swim away in search of easier prey. If the shark intensifies his or her efforts to rob you of energy, pay him or her a compliment. Redirect the conversation to a side topic that is related. Give a positive response reaffirming your boundaries. Or the shark, realizing that you are not giving away your energy, may swim away to find easier prey and that is OK too.

   A. **Breathe and be aware.**
   B. **Don't take it personally.**
   C. **Use the "Pause" button.**
   D. **Use energy shifters.**

E. Answer positively reaffirming your boundaries.
F. Smile and send energy.
G. Take care of yourself.

These are some suggested tools to use with sharks. Some may be more effective depending on the shark and situation you are in. Some tools may be more appropriate at work and others with friends. Experiment and try them out. See what works for you and comes most naturally to you. Or just use them all.

A. *Breathe and be aware.*

When a shark approaches you and barks or attacks, your first thought should be, "I'm going to breathe and pause. What is going on here? Is this a shark attack? I think so. There is no need for me to say or do anything at this moment." Just breathe. Take a pause to reflect on what is being said and how it is being said. Place yourself in the position of observer. What is the shark's purpose? Usually, it's to steal your energy. So, don't let that happen. Keep your cool while you think of which strategy (look below for ideas) you want to invoke. Or if you know you regularly swim with sharks, have one or two strategies ready to go so you are prepared. Preparation makes it easier to handle these situations.

B. *Don't take it personally.*

This is not about you. This situation in which you find yourself face to face with a shark is not about you. The shark was feeling insecure or vulnerable and was lacking energy so he or she went looking for energy prey. You just walked (or swam) into his or her path. It's not personal. This shark would find any prey to fit the bill.

Don Miguel Ruiz, author of **The Four Agreements**, wrote "When you make it a strong habit not to take anything personally, you avoid many upsets in your life. There is a huge amount of freedom that comes to you when you take nothing personally." (Ruiz, 1997) You can have so much more freedom when you don't take it personally. This is also great advice if you are the parent of a teenager. Just remember that it's not about you and the pain of the attack goes away. You can then resume your role as observer giving you a view with multiple options for a response.

C. Use the "Pause Button."

Sharks want you to immediately respond. They attack when you least expect it and then in that unguarded moment, you may do or say something that they can latch onto and start using to their advantage. Don't say anything. Don't do anything. Let there be an awkward, benevolent pause while you breathe and think and observe.

Every dolphin knows that there is an invisible pause button at his or her disposal for use at any time in any situation. Our society seems to think we need to answer every request, every question with an immediate answer via email or text or phone. This is not so. You can use the Pause button. This is important for dealing with a shark. You'll never give a shark a good enough answer when they are breathing down your neck. Tell them you'll get back to them in 10 minutes or an hour or some period of time that seems appropriate. Then you will have the time to breathe, think, and respond in an effective manner. And hold fast to your pause button. Sharks would like to take it away. Stand tall and tell them you will get back to them at such and such a time.

If the shark attack is more immediate and he or she is in your face, tell him or her you have to use the restroom or walk back to your office or their office. You may need time and space in order to form a decent response. Take it. Go breathe in the bathroom or while walking towards an office until you are calmer and can answer the question without your knees knocking or stumbling over your words. Sharks want the advantage of catching you by surprise so plan on that and be prepared before they attack. Know what tactic you will use to buy yourself more time. Usually, the shark will move on and attack someone else in the meantime because they did not get what they wanted from you. The more difficult you make it, the shark will respond by either trying harder or leaving you alone more often. So be ready for either response.

Hitting the PAUSE button is a very effective way of protecting your energy field so use it. You don't want the shark to steal all your energy leaving you listless for the rest of the day. It's like a bully stealing your lunch money. Protect yourself.

D. Use Energy Shifters

Ask a question. This is a great way of giving you more time to address the concern or attack of the shark. Ask a question to redirect the conversation or to get clarification but make sure there is no attitude in your voice. Be as neutral as you can. If you start to react with a defensive tone in your voice, you have grabbed their bait and they may as well suck all your energy dry immediately. Don't give them that pleasure. Ask a neutral question to stall and get your bearings. If you have to, you can pretend they are an ignorant, naïve child and you need to have patience and compassion to deal with them effectively. Find your nicest parent voice to use in this situation but don't be condescending just neutral.

Or sometimes you can surprise a shark by paying them a compliment. The shark is used to a certain script of how these situations go and paying a compliment breaks up the usual script. The shark expects a defensive remark from you from which they will continue their attack and get more aggressive to gather more energy from you. You are their current chosen victim. But if you reply in a non-conventional way by paying him or her a compliment, you may befuddle them. You are also giving them energy by paying them a compliment but you are in control of how much energy they get from you. You are still in control and are drawing boundaries for the shark. Be authentic in your compliment or the shark will smell something fishy and keep attacking. Say your compliment from your place of heart-centeredness and it will be most effective.

The use of humor is especially effective in shifting the energy of a shark. It makes them forget what they were doing in the first place. My son was being bullied on the soccer field, which was unusual for him as he is very tall for his age. They were telling him that he must be on steroids to be that tall and that he must be lying about his age. The bullies on the soccer team also acted out far too aggressively on the field. It was like playing a team of young sharks bent on these tactics to ruffle the feathers of our team so we couldn't focus on the game of soccer. That day it worked. My son was completely out of sorts and angry and beat up emotionally. We had a long talk about sharks and how to handle them. We came up with some one-liners to shoot back in a humorous way. When they said something snarky to him, he could say, "Yeah, I've heard that before" or "Oh, that's a good one." I'm sure there are better comebacks of a more humorous nature but I'm not that good at thinking them up. But you get the idea that humor, used correctly, can offset a shark's behavior and shift the energy. It can make you less desirable as a prey so they move on to someone else.

E. *Answer positively reaffirming your boundaries.*

The best way to explain this one is with an example. Let's say that your boss comes in yelling about a report that he should have had in his hands yesterday. You can reply with, "Yes, I will get that report to you by the end of the day." You are not explaining, backpedaling, justifying, defending, or anything else. You say yes. You tell him or her when you will get that report to them and then you follow up and do it. There is no need to have a lengthy conversation about this report. Answer the shark positively and reaffirm when they can expect the report from you. Don't add anything else to the conversation. Keep it really short and if that means a long, awkward pause after your response then so be it. Keep eye contact and smile just like a dolphin would. If you offer additional information or descriptions or apologies, the shark will smile and continue his attack as you just gave him additional ammunition. Keep it short and positive.

F. *Smile and send energy.*

Sometimes you can just smile and send love energy to this person who is just doing their best to get through life. Yes, I'm serious. They are glaring at you and you stand there calm and heart-centered with a smile on your face visualizing love all around them. It's easier to do if you imagine them as a small child, vulnerable and naïve. Smile a heart-centered smile and visualize a blanket of love traveling from deep within you over to them with no strings attached. You are doing this because you recognize this basic need inside of them to gather more energy and because you know a secret. You know that if they feel like they have enough energy, they will stop attacking or at least lessen the viciousness of their attacks and that's a good thing for you and everyone around you. Think about the possibility that if you give this shark enough energy doing this practice, he or she may not go around the entire office berating and attacking everyone within sight.

Plus, it really throws sharks off. They can't quite figure out what is going on and may just think you are weird. And if you're lucky, they may stop coming around so often because the attack is not really fun for them when you just smile. Or the opposite may occur. They may stop by your office and not even know why and you can just send them love and smile. That's really all they ever wanted from everyone. If you keep doing this practice, the shark might become less shark-like over time and that would be a great thing.

G. *Take care of you.*

Finally, what is most important is taking care of you. If you continually face a shark at work or on the PTA or with a group of friends, maybe you need to stop entering into the arena with the shark. Find another job or another department, find another group to volunteer with, or hang out with some dolphins. Walk away. Run away. Move away. Unless you get really used to handling sharks, it can wear on you over time. If you can learn to live like a dolphin, sometimes you can be a real influence on those around you. And if you become less carp like, the sharks around you may attack less often or stop it altogether. But be sure to take care of you even if that means less time with that person wearing the shark mask.

A Review

Let's go over what to do in case you meet up with a shark or a carp.

Encountering	Strategies	Things to Think and Say
a Carp	-Be mindful -Redirect the conversation -Bring energy to the group -Use energy shifters -If you have to carp, keep it short -Take care of yourself	What is going on? Is this a carp or a shark? What is my energy level like? Am I saying "I'm sorry" to this person? Get your energy up before entering the group and bring positive stories to share. Shake up the energy with humor, pay a compliment, or ask an unexpected question. Imagine a bubble of white light around you protecting your energy, center yourself in a gratitude practice, or excuse yourself to re-center for a few minutes before coming back. Leave when you need to or if you have to.

a Shark	-Breathe and be aware -Don't take it personally -Use the "Pause" button -Use energy shifters -Answer positively reaffirming your boundaries -Smile and send energy -Take care of yourself	When a shark barks at you, breathe and pause and pay attention to what is going on. You don't need to respond immediately. Keep your cool. Know that when a shark attacks, it's not personal. They are out to steal energy whether its yours or someone else's makes little difference to them. Recognize it for what it is. Let an awkward pause settle in before responding. Give yourself time to think. Tell them you'll get back to them in 5 minutes or 10. Give yourself time and space away from this person before you respond. Ask a question to redirect, pay a compliment, or invoke humor. Answer in a positive manner that tells this shark when and where and how you will get back to them. Keep it short and positive. The shark is after energy so send them a burst of energy and smile. It will help the interaction go better. Take care of yourself and your energy. Keep it up so that these shark attacks are more annoying than hurtful.

PART 2

Dolphin Behaviors

EVERY DOLPHIN CAN GET better at being a dolphin and spend more and more of their time living without masks. These behaviors are common to the dolphin. You may see some new ones that you might like to give a try. Adopting all of these behaviors brings more happiness, playfulness, lightness, and joy to your every day life and to the lives of those you love.

- Mindfulness
- Heart-Centered Living
- Know Your Values, Identity, and Boundaries
- Practice Gratitude and Identify Beauty
- Engage Intuition and Intention
- Live in Flow and Play in Joy
- Practice Acceptance and Care of Self and Others
- Be Authentic and Open
- Letting Go and Trusting the Universe
- Cooperation Over Competition

What you may not realize is that you are a spoke on a friendship/relationship wheel. Your energy and happiness affects the lives of all of those who are on your friendship/relationship wheel. When you are leading a more balanced, authentic, happier, and spiritually healthier life (spending more time as a dolphin), everyone around you benefits.

The research being done by Christakis and Fowler in their book, **Connected: The Surprising Power of Our Social Networks and How They Shape Our Lives**, supports this. They write, "Mathematical analyses of the network suggest that a person is about 15 percent more likely to be happy if a directly connected person (at least one degree of separation) is happy. And the spread of happiness doesn't stop there. The happiness effect for people at two degrees of separation (the friend of a friend) is 10 percent, and for people at three degrees of separation (friend of a friend of a friend), is about 6 percent." (Christakis & Fowler, 2009) Did you even know that friends of friends of friends being happy could boost your happiness? If you didn't think we were all connected before, does this start to change your mind? Happiness is contagious. Bring your happiness up a level and it affects everyone in your network of friends and family in a positive way.

Everyone on your friendship/relationship wheel gets a bump in his or her energy and happiness just by knowing you. Dolphins raise the energy and happiness quotient of everyone they come in contact with but especially the ones you love the most. Learn to be the dolphin for your own happiness knowing that this also helps the ones you love.

[5]

MINDFULNESS

DOLPHINS TAKE CARE OF their own energy. They know before they enter a room that they are responsible for the energy they bring into that space. They take that responsibility seriously so they stay attuned to their own energy level and know how to maintain and create energy to fulfill their energy needs. They check in with themselves throughout the day and see what their energy is like. Dolphins take a break and get themselves heart-centered again through whatever means works for them. If this means taking a walk in nature at lunchtime or a ten-minute meditation at their desk or in their car, they do it because they know it's important to themselves and those around them who they interact with. This awareness is the beginning of mindfulness.

Dolphins understand that no matter where they are, they are part of a pod and are in part responsible for the health of the entire pod. If their energy is off, then they are not contributing to the health of the pod. In fact, they are detracting from it. This pod could be their family, their co-workers, their charity organization, or their community depending on the day and time. The dolphin sees the importance of self-awareness and gets themselves back on track and reminds others to do the same if need be.

Dolphins use the strategy of **Stop – Observe — Reset** to get them back to being mindful and full of energy. I've heard many textbook definitions of what mindfulness is and what it isn't. Jon Kabat-Zinn, a leader in the field of mindfulness training, states that "mindfulness means **paying attention** in a particular way; **on purpose**, in the **present moment**, and **non judgmentally**." (Kabat-Zinn, 2005)

Deborah Schoeberlein and Suki Sheth in their book, **Mindful Teaching and Teaching Mindfulness**, write, "Mindfulness is a conscious, purposeful way of tuning in to what's happening in and around us.... The best of our human qualities, including the capacity for kindness, empathy, and compassion, support and are supported by mindfulness. Mindfulness and deep caring contribute to healthy relationships....Mindfulness is the means, and deep caring describes the manner." (Schoeberlein & Sheth, 2009) I applaud this definition as it points out that a part of mindfulness is caring and compassion. Sometimes it is difficult to define mindfulness in such narrow terms as our words allow. A real life example can offer more to the nuance of such an important concept so here goes.

My husband and I have five apartments that we own and manage and since my husband has the full-time career, I usually do the work involved with managing them. I'm not great at fixing up things but I do OK sometimes. A nice couple was moving in to our two-bedroom apartment in a few weeks and I had a few things to do while I oversaw the paint job and putting in new carpet, etc. While the painter was there, I thought I could install a new wireless doorbell. It's not difficult but I hadn't picked up a power drill in over a year.

I was in a hurry and just wanted to get it done before the appliance repairperson showed up. (Mistake #1 - not giving yourself enough time to complete the task.) I had the back of the button that you push for the doorbell and I needed to screw it into the wall outside the front door. I got one screw in and then the second one was giving me problems. I got mad. I was not breathing. I just wanted to get it done.

I jammed the drill into the remaining screw and pulled the trigger to turn the drill on full power as if my sheer willpower and brute force would fix it perfectly. (Obviously, this was the second mistake—not remaining calm).

Within a half a second, I stripped the screw and bent it at a 30-degree angle. Smoke was literally coming out of the drill as I pushed it so hard. And then...and then I reached out with my pointer finger and touched the top of the screw I just stripped. The screw was still smoking hot and burned a perfect circle into the pad of my pointer finger. OUCH! Oh my gosh! That hurt! Geez. What was I thinking?

Well, obviously, I was not thinking. This is what happens when you are not being mindful. I was not focused. I was not breathing. I was definitely NOT in the present moment. I was thinking about all the other things I had to get done and that the appliance guy was on his way and how I needed to get this done right away, etc. I was not paying attention to what I was doing or where my energy was. This was a perfect example of how NOT to practice mindfulness. Now, here's a positive example of mindfulness.

A week later, it was the day before this couple was supposed to move in. There were some crazy circumstances and a few miscommunications, which left me in a bind. I had to install five sets of new blinds, clean up the apartment, and take out all the trash by myself in a short amount of time. I knew this was an opportunity for me to practice mindfulness in action. I did not want to get hurt and I had to finish all these items in about four hours. I knew it was possible. Before I went over there, I made sure I had all the right tools and brought my lunch and water to keep my energy up. I also brought my puppy because I didn't want to leave him home all day plus he does a great job of keeping me company.

So, I already set myself up for success in terms of keeping my energy up which I believe is a crucial aspect of mindfulness. If my energy dips, I lose focus. I made sure to take care of my physical needs for the time I would be spending there with food, drink, a chair, and access to a restroom. I brought the right tools and had everything I needed to complete the tasks. I also brought music to listen to so I could keep my energy up and make it fun.

I took a deep breath and let it out relaxing my shoulders and preparing to go slow and steady through these sets of blinds. I chose my first set and began the steps needed to complete it. Each movement was slow and deliberate. I moved the ladder and made sure it was stable. I grabbed the tools I needed and put screws in my pockets and thought about each move before I did it. I breathed into each step and laid the power drill (yes, the same one I used before when I burned my finger) very carefully on the top of the ladder each time I put it down. I made sure to take it down from the ladder each time so it wouldn't just fall on the hundred-year-old wood floor or break the window if I bumped the ladder.

When I was tired, I sat down on the chair and loved on my dog for a while. I drank some water. I took some breaths and relaxed my body. I would tell myself I was doing a great job. I admired my work. It was a dance—a dance of mindful thoughts, words, and actions to move forward slowly but surely.

Then I would get back up and do the next set of blinds. After two sets of blinds, I ate my lunch. After three sets of blinds, I texted a picture of my good work to my husband for some positive feedback. It was a complete exercise in mindfulness. I kept my cool. When I had a problem, I stopped. I thought about it patiently. I checked with my intuition. I breathed. When I found a solution I thought would work, I patiently began to work on it and to my relief, I was successful. I continued slowly, deliberately, and breathed in and out with focus and mindfulness. I was paying attention. I was in the present moment. I was on purpose. This felt good.

The work hours went by quickly and even though I was very tired and a bit sweaty, I was mentally still very focused and balanced. I almost finished everything. I still had one set of blinds to pick up at the home improvement store but I had to pick up my son at school as well. So, I breathed into the situation and calmed myself down. I looked for a solution and decided I would ask for help. This is also an important thing to be able to do. I had done well but was too tired to keep going at this point.

So, I decided to get my son from school, take a break at home, and then ask my husband to come back with me later to finish. I could have decided to muscle through and tough it out by picking up my son and coming right back to finish but I knew that the work would not be mindful anymore. If I had continued, I might have gotten hurt or made mistakes that would cost me more time and money. I was done at that moment and needed a break so I wisely didn't go back right away.

I came back a few hours later with my husband and we finished it up in 45 minutes, together. I was so glad I did because that last set of blinds was a bit of a challenge and I would not have had the energy to complete it by myself. I was very wise to ask for help.

The next day, the couple happily moved in and I was proud because the apartment looked fabulous and I was not mentally or physically drained. I had taken care of myself and my energy. I had no resentment built up because I had to work so hard the day before. I felt good and because my energy was good, the couple felt that and were extremely happy to move into this wonderful apartment full of good energy.

I hope this example of mindfulness (and non-mindfulness) in the real world helps make the concept clearer and easier to understand. I used mindfulness to flow through my day, make good decisions, and got a heck of a lot of work done quickly and well. I made no mistakes.

I didn't make any extra work for myself either. It was efficient and actually enjoyable.

I've tried to make checking in a habit. I check in several times a day and especially before starting any home improvement projects. I try to ask myself these questions: What's my energy level? Am I being mindful?

So how do you make this a habit? You can start by setting up random timers on your smartphone throughout the day. Just have them go off at weird intervals throughout your day with the question, "What is your energy level?" or "Are you being mindful?" These will serve as reminders to check your mindfulness and energy level throughout the day.

Another way to start a mindfulness habit is to start checking on your energy level before meeting friends and family or before every meeting at work or before entering your house at the end of the day. Find points of time where it is most beneficial or most convenient to check in with yourself. If you pick up your child from school every day, check your energy before you pick him or her up. Make sure you are in a good space to be there for your child. Those drives in the car can be important to developing your relationship but if your energy is low, you can't be in a good space to make that conversation count. And check to see that you are being mindful as well. Are you in the present moment with the people you are talking to? Are you focused on the task at hand? Are you taking care of yourself?

Another way that I've become aware of my energy is through my body. It sends off many signals if you just become aware of them and pay attention. Look for tightness or stiffness. Does your body feel relaxed or constricted? If your gut is wrenching (feeling tight), then something is seriously wrong in your environment. Do a survey and take note of what is going on. Your body is trying to talk to you. I was watching a TV show with my husband and son when I noticed that my gut was clenched to the point of almost making me sick. I hadn't really been paying attention. Finally, when I thought about it, I realized that I didn't like the message of this show for my young son and I didn't want him watching it. I shared this with my husband and son and we immediately switched shows to something lighter and more age appropriate. My gut wrench went away. This is another important part of mindfulness. This awareness is crucial for maintaining your balance and staying centered. Your body is just another tool for tuning in. Pay attention.

Checking in with your body is also an excellent way to check your own energy level. Are you yawning? Feeling like you could crawl under your desk for a nap? Again, these are obvious signs that your energy is low and that could just be a lack of sleep or it could mean that you could benefit from a push on the reset button on your MegaEnergyTron.

And then the most telling sign that I need something to change with my current energy level is when I reply to someone in snarky, angry, or exasperated tones (Oh yes, this happens from time to time. Just ask my husband or son.) When I am cranky, that is a clear indication that I need to do something different and push my own Reset button. My son is now tuned in as well and when I am cranky or speak roughly to him, he can look at me and suggest I go meditate. This jars me out of my crankiness and I thank him and proceed to my office to meditate. My husband will also suggest it and as a dolphin, I appreciate that. I don't get angry at them for the suggestion. I know they want the happy, lovable and centered Melinda to come back and that's the fastest way for me to get there.

A dolphin realizes that no one else is going to do this for them. Others can remind us of what needs to be done but only we can go and do it. Dolphins remind themselves that they are responsible for their own energy. They are responsible for the energy they bring to every situation in their life. You can't count on someone to come along and make you laugh every time you are down, although that would be nice.

Using this strategy of staying aware of one's own energy level (staying mindful) gets the dolphin back to living in the present moment. Resetting their energy level keeps them from dwelling on the past or worrying about the future and centers them in the gift of now.

A NOTE TO EMPATHS

What is an empath? I didn't know for a long time that I was an empath. When I first worked in an office day in and day out when I was 23 years old, I had no idea that I was picking up everyone else's energies and taking them home with me each night. I would find myself upset or crying or angry for no reason at all. I never could seem to control my emotions. I was up. I was down. I was on a roller coaster ride every day. I took on other people's emotions to please them so if they were angry, I would take that away for them and then carry their anger around. I was quite a people pleaser so I took on EVERYONE's STUFF. I took on whatever emotion was burdening them and took it home with me. That was not a great time in my life. I don't know how my husband put up with me, frankly. After some time at home, I would reset and find myself again but I wasn't meditating. I was not being mindful. I was just confused. I was kind of miserable at my job just because I was taking on everyone else's emotional baggage.

An empath is sensitive to the emotional needs and the energy of others around them. They are often intuitive and may unconsciously be influenced by other people's moods, desires, or thoughts. Empaths can tell what other people are thinking or feeling. I remember sitting in work meetings and just knowing what one person was thinking while another one was presenting an idea. I could translate between people who couldn't understand each other very well. I could do all of that without thinking about it. If this sounds like you, you may be an empath. I suggest you look this up and research a bit about being it. It can be a difficult path for some when there is no awareness of what is going on. I speak from experience.

If you think you might be an empath, you will want to practice mindfulness and energy awareness with vigor. Your emotional state and your energy may be at the whim of those around you and that is not a good thing. Take back control of your own emotional state and balance by understanding energy maintenance and creation as discussed earlier in this book. You will want to practice placing an invisible bubble around yourself each day to protect your energy and to help you start identifying what is your emotional stuff and what is the emotional stuff of the people around you. You will start to be able to tell the difference. It's not your responsibility to take on other people's problems on an energetic level. That will drain you and not allow you to be centered and balanced in your own life.

One trick I've learned is cord cutting. You visualize your bubble of energy and light around you and use your intuition to "see" if there are people with cords reaching into your bubble and stealing energy from you. You can imagine a big pair of scissors going around the outside of your bubble cutting all these cords away. This will leave you with an insulated energy bubble around you. This may seem like just a mumbo jumbo visualization exercise but I speak from personal experience that this works. I've made tremendous progress towards more peace and happiness by engaging this technique (often at first and now just every once in awhile).

Summing Up

Mindfulness begins with an awareness of your energy level. You can then proceed to reset your energy if you need to. Then you can proceed forward in a mindful, focused way while breathing and taking care of yourself. Checking in throughout the day as to your energy level helps you keep your energy level up and consistent so you don't go cranky. Resetting your energy level is an individual thing and you need to figure out what works for you. A few minutes of meditation or just sitting in nature are excellent ways to begin your mindfulness practice.

[6]

HEART-CENTERED LIVING

IN MY EXPERIENCE, OUR society places a tremendous value on the mind—its logic and problem-solving abilities. Every person wants to be smart and use his or her head. But in looking around our world, I think we could use a little more balance between the head and the heart. We would all think that Albert Einstein most encompasses the model of using his brain, his logic, and his problem-solving skills. But the more I read his writings, the more I'm surprised as he wrote, "Don't let your brain interfere with your heart." Even Einstein recognized the importance of your sidekick, the hearSo what do we know about the heart? Is it just emotion? Is it wild and uncontrollable? Or is there more to it than that? I say there is much, much more. In the book, **The HeartMath Solution** by Doc Childre and Howard Martin, they have developed a comprehensive system for accessing this heart intelligence. These authors write, "The heart isn't mushy or sentimental. It's intelligent and powerful, and we believe that it holds the promise for the next level of human development and for the survival of our world." (Childre, Martin, & Beech, 1999)

The power of the dolphin comes from his or her mindfulness working in conjunction with the divine intelligence of the heart. Accessing this heart intelligence is huge and life changing in every way. I've accessed a new happier way of living and way of moving through this chaotic world by engaging my heart. Childre and Martin describe it this way, "Heart intelligence is the intelligent flow of awareness and insight that we experience once the mind and emotions are brought into balance and coherence through a self-initiated process. This form of intelligence is experienced as direct, intuitive knowing that manifests in thoughts and emotions that are beneficial for ourselves and others." (Childre, Martin, & Beech, 1999) This is what I call heart-centeredness for the dolphin. Balancing the heart and mind in an intelligent flow of intuitive action is at the heart of being a dolphin.

The authors go on to explain that the heart is more than just a 10-ounce pump that circulates our blood until we die. Did you know that the heart starts beating in a fetus before the brain has been formed? How does it know when to begin beating? Is there intelligence there? Childre and Martin write that neuroscientists have discovered that the heart has its own independent nervous system or a "brain in the heart." They have discovered that there are at least 40,000 neurons inside the heart. The heart actually sends messages to the brain. (Childre, Martin, & Beech, 1999)

So, maybe that advice to "listen to your heart" was not that far off. Ralph Waldo Emerson wrote, "What your heart thinks is great, is great. The soul's emphasis is always right." Think about cultures around the world and how often they mention the heart. The heart was central to the Egyptians in their burial rites. Ancient cultures around the world discuss the heart and its uniqueness. Even in the Bible from the Old Testament, "For as a man thinketh in his heart, so is he." (Zondervan, 2010) In New Age practices, the chakra system contains the heart chakra in the center with 3 chakras above and 3 below. Many meditations center on the heartbeat to calm yourself down and begin to focus. These ancient traditions appear to be are way more in touch with what scientists are just unraveling today.

Maybe there's much more going on with the heart than we ever thought possible.

I learned a long time ago about listening to that still, small voice inside but it's only been in the last several years that I've been paying more attention to the heart. Now I know that this still, small voice resides inside the heart. This is your spidey sense. This is the voice that steps in when you are about to make a decision and suddenly stops you and makes you not feel right about it. There is logic in your decision but the heart may suggest something's not right. I've finally decided to listen to that little voice inside of me and it's made all the difference. This is where intuition starts—in the heart. I've been practicing living in the heart for the past few years and it's shifted my life in amazing ways. I'm happier and more content than ever before and my relationships are more satisfying and rewarding than I ever thought possible. This is all from living from the heart and it's nice that the research in **The HeartMath Solution**, by Childre and Martin, confirms all of this for my inquisitive, logical mind as well. (Childre, Martin, & Beech, 1999)

I like to use the word "heart-centeredness" when I need to describe my experience of intuition to others. There is a deep richness and flavor to the intuition gained when you are heart-centered. I have felt this deep well of compassion and love in my meditation practice and in my intuitive work with clients. There is a divine intelligence there and now I know exactly where it resides. Now I can work with it on a conscious level instead of in an unconscious unfocused way.

When I use my intuition or do Tarot card readings for friends and family, I access deep, divine heart intelligence and when you do that, you find this space where only integrity and compassion and non-judgment lives. You see other people as an extension of yourself and you only want to help them find their way. You want to help them find deep peace and understanding of their place in the universe. When you are accessing this heart intelligence, there is only love and there is no place for trickery or manipulation. It is pure love and a higher vibration than you can imagine. And not only do you access your intuition but you heal your body and regulate your heartbeat and emanate this deep peace out to everyone you meet that day. What could be more beautiful than that? This is the essence of the dolphin. There is no judgment, only a deep well of love and wisdom that guides the dolphin in his or her daily actions. This is what living from the heart looks and feels like.

Living from your heart-center not only helps you physically and emotionally but you'll have intuition that will help you make decisions that will benefit your life. How cool is that? It's not woowoo. It's just what is. I think it's the next evolution of humankind. I think it's how we are supposed to work or maybe it's how we used to function thousands of years ago before we forgot.

When we can balance the logic of our minds with the innate intelligence of our hearts, we can be the dolphin. We need to start listening to the heart. It has a lot to say. It's time for us to step into this new way of living—living from the heart. As Childre and Martin put it, "As science continues to discover how people can harness and direct the coherent power of the heart, it offers tremendous hope that society can shift from disorder and chaos to a new era of coherence and quality living for all." (Childre, Martin, & Beech, 1999, p. 4)

Carl Jung wrote "Your vision will become clear only when you look into your heart ... Who looks outside, dreams. Who looks inside, awakens." Awaken that dolphin that lives within you.

So, let's get real about how this looks in every day life. I don't get angry very often but a few days ago, I did. Like I said, I'm a work in progress and being a dolphin most of the time doesn't mean you don't make mistakes or have emotional outbursts. My son didn't have any homework and I decided I wanted him to help me with dinner and read for 30 minutes instead of just playing videogames or cruising social media that whole time. I started making a dinner that takes a long time to make (fried chicken from scratch and mashed potatoes and gravy). I asked my son to peel the potatoes. He put up such a fight. You'd think that I was asking him to clean the bathroom floor with a toothbrush. He complained and whined the entire time saying the peeler was digging into his skin and how bad he was at it. I tried to be encouraging and told him he'd get better at it the more he did it. That didn't really help. In the end, I was annoyed. He finished and I had to sigh and ask myself whether that was even worth it. I didn't say anything to him about his attitude and that was my first mistake.

I went on with making dinner and reiterated my request that he read for 30 minutes by the time dinner was ready at 7pm. He whined and complained about that as well. I set boundaries by telling him that if he didn't read for 30 minutes, the consequence would be no TV show that night. He murmured something like an acknowledgement as he continued looking at his phone.

Time goes by and I see that it's 6pm and he hasn't moved to pick up his book. It's 6:15 and then 6:30pm. I try to remind him nicely that he should probably pick up that book sometime soon. He glares at me with that glare that only teenagers can manage. I leave it alone and let the consequences fall where they may but I fail to notice that my anger and annoyance level has ratcheted up. I am no longer mindful or calm. I am truly annoyed that I am being so blatantly ignored in my request. He won't finish his 30 minutes of reading by 7pm unless he starts now. Ugh. Then he'll be upset because he doesn't get to watch the family TV show and my husband and I will be annoyed too because we enjoy that time together. It's now 6:45pm and I have to say something. "You know, you're never going to finish 30 minutes of reading by 7pm." "WHAT? You didn't say I had to finish BY 7pm!" Insert giant parental sigh here. He wasn't listening to the details of my request. Now what do I do? I told him that I made it very clear and he just sat there continuing to play on this phone. I told him I was mad because now he was going to be upset that he wasn't getting to watch his movie and none of us could watch. And now I didn't even want the dinner I had spent all of this time making because I was angry. [Not my best moment but there you have it.]

   I turned off the TV and walked off. I was quite angry. I knew I needed some space and going outside was probably a good idea in this moment. [Here is a winning moment for me as a parent.] I recognized that I needed to hit the PAUSE button and RESET. I went out to the front porch realizing that I needed to breathe and take in some nature. I was a bit tired from making a time intensive dinner and I had already had to fight my son to get him to peel the potatoes. I had not sat down in an hour and a half. I was not taking care of myself. I was not heart-centered. I breathed into the early evening cool air. I relaxed my shoulders. I looked up into the sky and attempted to reset my energy. I thought about the clouds, took in the soft evening light of sunset, and listened to the birds still singing despite the hour. All of these things brought me back to myself—to my heart-centered self. The tension in my shoulders and my gut eased and relaxed. I could think more clearly.

   I looked back over the situation with my son and realized that I didn't want to feel this sense of separation from him, which my judgment of him had created. I didn't want the evening to be awful because of this one thing that went wrong. I wanted to enjoy the delicious dinner I had prepared and have all of us enjoy family time around the table. Yes, that was what I wanted. How was I going to get there? How could I still uphold boundaries with my son and yet get back to a connected, heart-centered state? I breathed some more and felt ready to go back inside.

   My son was dutifully reading his book. From my heart, I asked for an apology, which he quickly gave. I still wasn't 100% heart-centered so I should have gone back out and meditated for a few minutes. If I had, I would have then apologized for getting angry. That didn't happen then because as I said, I am a work in progress.

[I did apologize for my getting angry later on, just so you know.] But instead of my son losing his TV show that evening (an episode of "Dr. Who") which was the consequence for not reading for 30 minutes before dinner, we negotiated that he would read an extra 10 minutes after dinner and that would be that. We would move forward as dolphins. My heart and my body were in alignment with this agreement and so was his.

We enjoyed the good dinner with my husband who got home right after that. My son read for his 10 extra minutes. After he read that extra 10 minutes, I could then let go of most of my anger. It just took me a little longer than it would have if I had meditated straight away. But I knew that when I came inside, I was in a much better place and I did have to get dinner on the table so there was no time for a meditation right then. Sometimes that is necessary. The rest of the evening was pleasant as we all enjoyed a great episode of "Dr. Who" together. There was no need to carry the anger into the rest of the evening. Better to get reset by enjoying nature and breathing for a few minutes to get back to being heart-centered (if not 100% then at least 70%).

This is what a dolphin does. A dolphin watches his or her energy and takes action when it needs to be reset. Make it a priority to get back to being heart-centered. I know I'm back to being heart-centered when I can look upon my son with love in my eyes and my heart and be thankful that he is in my life. If I can't do that, I'm not back to being 100% heart-centered and more action is required on my part. If I came back inside and I wasn't heart-centered at all, how do you think the rest of that evening would have gone? Would there have been any apologies? Would an easy resolution have come about that we both felt good about? Would the dinner have tasted good if I was still angry? How would the dinner conversation be? Being angry is not worth losing an opportunity to connect with loved ones over a delicious dinner, right? You can consciously choose in every moment to make it a good, loving moment or be full of anger and righteousness and make everyone else suffer. I could have chosen to be angry for three days. It was all my choice and we all make these choices every day.

This checking in on your heart and body is so important. Just before we started "Dr. Who," I still felt a tightness in my stomach and knew that there was still something bothering me. I was still not 100% heart-centered yet. I focused on what had happened and became aware of one more thing I wanted to say about the situation to my son. Earlier in the afternoon, I had asked for help with peeling the potatoes for dinner and my son complied kicking and screaming and whining the whole time. I didn't say anything at the time and that was my mistake. But I still felt resentment and anger about that incident and I didn't want to go to bed with that in my belly. I still wasn't 100% heart-centered or what I would call "clean" with my energy.

So, I breathed into my heart and asked for my son's attention. I calmly said, "You know how you acted when I asked you to peel potatoes and the whining that came while you were doing it, I want you to know that I don't appreciate that. In the future, I'd really like it if you could just pitch in and help when I ask. I work really hard on preparing good, slow food for us and I could use your help when you don't have homework." He got the point and said, "OK. Sorry Mom." When you speak from a heart-centered space, people listen, even teenagers. When you speak from anger, they don't hear a thing. Upon sharing how I felt, my resentment lifted, my stomach muscles relaxed, and I was ready to be 100% heart-centered again.

Setting Boundaries and "Clean" Energy

I was being heart-centered in that I was setting boundaries that were comfortable for me so that my energy would stay positive and not fall into resentment. If I had not spoken up for how I wanted my son to treat me, what would have happened the next time I asked him to help with dinner and he again was whining and complaining? Would my anger be even more intense? Would I harbor resentment? Would I be a martyr and not even ask him to help me and just be quietly resentful and passively aggressive towards him? These are all choices open to me. I have learned that holding onto anger does not work for me. I like my energy "clean" where I am ready to love with all of my heart and bear no resentment towards my loved ones. Does that make sense? This is also a definition of living in a heart-centered manner.

Do you see in this example how setting boundaries and asking for people to treat you with respect leads to heart-centeredness? When you don't let people know something is bothering you, it can lead to resentment and anger. If I had told my son that his attitude toward peeling potatoes was inappropriate when it was happening and maybe do it in a gentle, funny way, maybe I wouldn't have had such an angry response when he didn't listen to me about reading for 30 minutes. But I let the potato peeling behavior go and it festered. It made it easier to get angry just a few minutes later. You see, I have a pattern of doing that in my life. I let things go and don't say anything to make it easier for everyone else (People Pleasing 101) but then after several things happen in a row that annoy or anger me, I would blow up and get super angry. And my angry response was way bigger than the latest annoyance so my overblown response confused my loved ones. They couldn't figure out why I was so upset over the tiniest thing. But it wasn't that I was upset over that tiny thing. It was that I was upset over the ten or twenty things before that when I never said anything. That is **my** bad. I take responsibility for that.

People can't change their behavior if they don't even know it bothers you. You are responsible for letting them know. That is another way of being heart-centered that you may not have thought about before. Being heart-centered means that you let people know when things bother you so you don't blow up and get angry at the tiniest thing. You can be even keel and heart-centered more of the time when you share what you need and want in your relationship every day in every way. Not sharing these simple little things leads to not being heart-centered. Do you see that?

When you share what bothers you, you are transparent. You are more authentic. People can trust that they are in your good graces if you share when things they do actually bother you. Because they know if you are not sharing that anything is bothering you, they must be doing OK. If you never tell someone that something bothers you or only share occasionally or just drop hints, people don't know if they can trust that you are truly OK with what they are doing and how they are treating you. This leads to icky energy between you. Icky energy is not heart-centeredness. It's not "clean" energy. Sharing and being open allows for "clean" energy to exist in your relationship leading the way to more heart-centered interactions. Sharks are not transparent and will engage in passive-aggressive behaviors when they don't share that things are bothering them. Do you see that? Sharks will say something snarky that you are left to interpret and figure out that something you are doing is bothering them. But you are never quite sure what it is. It just feels terribly muddy. Carp may say something like, "Oh, I guess I'll just peel the potatoes AGAIN" in their best martyr voice. Instead, they could ask you to help peel the potatoes but they don't. They skirt around it. Being a dolphin means asking for what you want and being transparent in your requests of others and how you want to be treated. Is that starting to make sense?

WARNING

When I first began cleaning the energy with my close loved ones, I think I was a bit too angry. I had let things fester for too long. If you think this might be the case with you, try to prioritize your list of how you want to be treated and then limit your sharing of something that bothers you to one thing a week or every few weeks. Don't dump them on the other person all at one time. That is not fair and it is not heart-centered to do that. You need to take responsibility for not having shared that these things bothered you from the very beginning. That is on you. So, find your heart-center and share one thing at a time when it feels intuitively right to do so. You are re-teaching others how to treat you and this takes time and patience on your part and theirs. Show them compassion as they learn what you need in the relationship. Allow them the space and time to move and adapt to this new situation. Doing it all at once doesn't help anyone. I know. I made that mistake too. And be open if they too want to "clean" the energy with how you treat them too. They may find their dolphin side as well and you will need to be gracious and accommodating of their needs as well.

More On Heart-Centeredness

When you are heart-centered, you feel as if you want to do what is best for everyone and you are generous and loving to your very core. There is no ego, no sense of greed just an innate knowing that there is enough for everyone. It's a relaxed feeling of love in your heart. Decisions are clear and lead to a sense of freedom when based in love. Grace and flow accompany this state of heart-centeredness. As you learn to see what this state feels like, you'll be able to get there faster. You'll learn what works to get you to this heart-filled way of being.

There are many paths to heart-centeredness and everyone is unique on how they want to travel there. I know for me one of the fastest ways for me to get heart-centered is gratitude. I start listing all the things, people, and situations I am grateful for. I feel into them and get real about how blessed and thankful I am for all the good in my life. That turns me around and gets me heart-centered very quickly but you will learn what works for you. You may have several modes for getting heart-centered. I know that meditation also works well for me as does being in nature. Be flexible, try things out, and find new ways to get even deeper into your heart center. It is a better way of living that leads to more happiness for you and for those you love. Being heart-centered also means taking action sometimes to get there. When I was working on that situation with my son, I had to breathe, go outside in nature, look at the situation, feel into my gut, and share how I wanted my son to treat me. Being heart-centered always requires action on your part. You just have to be heart smart about the best way to get there.

HEART-CENTERED COMMUNICATION

Life is messy and relationships are fluid. Being heart-centered can help guide you and navigate the waters of love in a way that strengthens rather than tears down your relationships. Whenever there is a serious conversation to be had within a relationship, it is in your best interest to get heart-centered first. There are times when you need to share something that bothers you in the relationship and the only way—the ONLY WAY—the other person will be able to hear you is if you speak from this space of heart-centeredness. Some ways to do this are to find a quiet space where you won't get interrupted and sit down with your loved one. You can begin the conversation by saying something like, "It really hurts my feelings and makes me feel awful when...." Be more curious in how to resolve the situation than in dictating a solution. Your loved one might surprise you with a resolution you had not previously thought of.

Make sure your communication is clear, heart-centered, and specific. Don't use this time to share judgments you have about your loved one and make them feel bad. Don't engage in name-calling. Don't use this as a time to bring up every single thing that has bothered you over the past year or five years. This is the start of a heart-centered communication bridge that you can return to at a later time. Start with the most recent thing that is bothering you. If you make it about twenty things, that is not being heart-centered and your partner will not hear you. Instead, share how you feel in a heart-centered way about this specific thing and ask how to avoid this in future situations. Maybe it's just having the other person realize that this action hurts you and they will try to not do it in the future. That might be all that is needed.

And remember that relationships are a two-way street. By opening up this safe, communication bridge (maybe it's the first time you've ever done this), be ready if your partner opens up to you about something that has been bothering them. Listen. Respond with love. Accept that this is how they are feeling. You don't get to decide how they are feeling or what things should make them feel one way or another. Feelings are not wrong. They just are. They feel what they feel just as you feel what you feel. Be open and heart-centered and ready to listen to what they need from you. Come up with solutions together. Apologize if it seems appropriate. Share that you truly love them, want to support them, and not hurt them. This leads to deeper connection, less resentment, and more heart-centeredness all around. And creating this safe space for communication keeps the energy in your relationship "clean." Having one of these conversations for the first time can be awkward so just let it be that. It's OK. You'll get better at it—both of you. And it will get a bit easier. But knowing you have this safe space for heart-centered communication makes it so much easier to move through both easy and difficult times together.

Heart-Centered Meditation

To open up to your heart center during meditation, you can follow along with these ideas.

When you start your meditation, focus on one time in your life when you felt big love for the earth. Maybe it was a time at the beach or putting your feet into a cold, mountain stream. But feel into that memory and give thanks to Mother Earth by focusing a white light straight down from the bottom of your feet down through the soil and rock straight down to the center of the earth. This white light connects and grounds you into the energy of this planet. Then Mother Earth sends the white light back up to you through the rock and the soil to the bottom of your feet where it travels up through your body energizing you. The white light travels from the bottom of your feet all the way up through your spine filling you with light. It comes out the top of your head and travels up through the atmosphere into the universe up to your own personal white star in the cosmos. You feel the trail of white light from the center of the earth up to your white star in the heavens above. The white star returns the bright, healing white light back down to you through the top of your head, through your body, and back down into Mother Earth. This visualization strengthens your connection to all that is and with each breath you take, this connection stays strong and vital.

Then imagine a beautiful green light coming from your heart center. It begins as a tiny point of light and gradually expands getting bigger and bigger and then becomes a giant bubble of love and green light surrounds you and comes from your heart. You feel a deep love for all things as this green light pulses and sweeps out any negative thoughts or feelings. You feel generous and peaceful as you allow this green light to be inside and around you filling everyone and everything with love. Know that this love is endless, limitless, and fills you with love. And as you move through your day, this bubble of green light around you touches those you come in contact with and fills them with love also. Give thanks for this day, this life, and know that you are loved always.

Heart-Centered Activity Ideas

Here are some ideas on how to get heart-centered. Please list your own below so you think about it and have them ready to go when you need to reset.

1. Sit in nature and take in the beauty of a tree, a flower, the song of a bird, or the shape of the clouds.
2. Think of ten things you are grateful for and sit with those feelings of deep gratitude. Realize that your life even with its problems and complexities is so much better than so many other people living on this planet right now. You have a bed, food, a state of peace in this country, access to drinking water, a shower, etc. There really is so much to be thankful for and this practice can get you back into a heart-centered space.
3. Meditation works well. You can practice on your own with some peaceful music or download some guided meditations to get you started. If you have never practiced meditation before, you might want to visit a site like headspace.com where they guide you through the process.
4. Do something creative. Play music, dance around, sing loudly, paint a picture, color, cook, write a song or a poem, create a new move in soccer or basketball, or just play like you are five years old. Engage your little kid self and do something that makes you laugh or feel silly. You can't be laughing and not feel heart-centered.
5. Engage beauty. Appreciate some art, listen to music, watch children play, seek out animals, take in the view, arrange some flowers, or do something that touches your heart because it's so beautiful.

What is on your list that will help you get heart-centered?

_____
_____
_____

[7]

Know Your Values, Identity, & Boundaries

DOLPHINS ARE VERY CLEAR on what their values are and what they stand for. When I was in middle school, I had to memorize quotes and one of them was "If you don't stand for something, you will fall for anything." It's so true. Getting clear on what is important to you helps you clarify your identity and transmit that clearly to everyone you meet.

Have you ever met someone and said, "Wow. This guy is so honest. It just comes through in everything he says and how he holds himself." That is someone who knows what he stands for and transmits it clearly to everyone he meets. The Dalai Lama is a great example of this. I was fortunate enough to hear him when he toured the world for his 80th birthday in 2015. He so clearly transmitted compassion. He lived and breathed compassion for every human being so clearly and enthusiastically that everyone in that huge auditorium could feel it. It's difficult to put the feeling into words but you know it when you feel it. When a person is very clear on what they value and what they stand for, it shines in everything they do and say. This is what dolphins do.

Identifying your values can help you more clearly delineate who you are so you can share that with others. In addition, it helps you choose the path before you with greater confidence. If you know that honesty, responsibility, and being joyful are what make you tick, then you can weigh any decision against those three values to make a choice. Does that decision align with your values? If you say yes to that decision, will you feel honest, responsible, and joyful? It's much easier to make that decision if you know what values you uphold. The path ahead becomes clearer and you may find that the opportunities begin to line up with the values you hold dear. Transmitting who you are clearly attracts more of that to you. If you hold love as the bottom line, then you will attract more opportunities related to valuing love and sharing love with the world.

Values are part of what makes you who you are. Being clear on that means that you are clearer on your identity. And if you are clear on your identity then other people are too. You can attract people who are more like you and who value what you do when you are very clear about who you are. Does that make sense?

If you value gentleness, respect, and appreciating beauty and you want to find a partner who understands that, isn't it in your best interest to transmit that with every fiber of your being? It's like putting out a mating call that only those who value what you do, will answer. That's important, no?

Another very important part of being a dolphin is creating boundaries around who you are and what you will tolerate from others in terms of their treatment of you. We touched on this in the chapter on Heart-Centeredness. Dolphins understand that the word, "No" is a complete sentence. They feel free to say yes or no to whatever request comes their way. They know that real, true friends will appreciate that when they say "Yes" they really mean it and that when they say "No" that their friends will still be their friends. Saying "No" is not a rejection. It is simply "No, I can't do that right now." There is no additional hidden message to the "No." There is no undercurrent. When dolphins communicate with each other, there is no hidden agenda. There is no resentment. It is a transparent, heart-centered communication. If there were anything additional to be said, it would be shared. You can trust a dolphin to say what he or she means.

I went through the first 35 years of my life as a people pleasing carp that said yes to almost every request and then was filled with resentment and anger afterwards. I'd get so mad at someone for asking me to do something because then I'd have to say "Yes" or feel very guilty about saying "No." Then I'd be afraid that person wouldn't like me anymore if I said no to them. Or if I said yes and didn't really want to do whatever was being asked, then I'd procrastinate, have a poor attitude about it, or do a poor job of it, which wasn't really how I wanted to show up in the world. I was not clear on who I was or what I valued and I didn't value myself enough to hold strong to boundaries and say "No" when I wanted to. People couldn't trust that I was telling the truth and that I meant "Yes" when I said "Yes." And that's hard for dolphins because then they have to second-guess whether you really mean "yes" or whether you are just saying that because you have weak boundaries. The energy around asking a people pleasing carp to do something can become yucky and cloudy. Some dolphins may just stay away because they don't know how to handle a carp's boundaries and they don't want to enter into sticky energy like that. They want "clean" energy interactions as discussed in the chapter on Heart-Centeredness.

It all starts with valuing yourself. You have to know that you are of value. You are loved. You are a valuable part of this world or you wouldn't be here. You are needed at this time in this place. It's important that you show up as your true, authentic dolphin self. You can be a light to others in the darkness of this existence. It is so important. You are so important. Do you get that? We need everyone to show up and be his or her own unique and beautiful self. That is the only way this world will become a better place. And yes, I am speaking to you.

Now let's get to setting boundaries. Setting a boundary means that you count. When the PTA calls to ask you to bring cupcakes and juice boxes to the next event for the 37th time this year on a week when you know you've got too many other responsibilities, you politely say "No, I can't do it this week." There is no need to explain why. Let your answer stand. Don't submit to any complaints on the other end of the line. Hold your ground and know that this is what is best for you in this moment—to say "No" politely and steadfastly. If the person on the other end of the line gets mad at you, so be it. If that person doesn't speak to you again, they are not worth knowing.

You deserve to have people around you who understand that sometimes you need to say "No" to keep yourself from being stretched too thin. You need to take care of yourself. The person on the other end of the phone may not know that you are starting a new business, writing a book, taking care of sick children, or caring for an aging parent and that is where you need to focus your time. Other dolphins will take your "No" and be glad that you are taking care of what you need to take of. Because if you are taking care of you, that means the whole pod is healthier as a result and they can find someone else to do whatever it was they asked you to do. Do you get it?

When you connect to the universal source of energy to fill you up, there is no need for you to gain the approval of others to give you a boost of energy, which is what you do when you say "yes" but want to say "no." There is no need to "people please" quite so much as you felt before. You have your own gas station in the sky for getting energy. You don't need to say "Yes" to get validated as a person. You know what values you stand for and you know you are a valued and loved person because you are here right now on planet Earth and that is enough. There is no need for any outer validation. It is enough that

Know Your Values, Identity, & Boundaries | 129

you are here now as a human being beginning to stand in the power of love.

To take this a step further, begin to become aware of how others treat you. How do you let others treat you? Do you let them criticize you? Do you let them tear you down? Do you let them build you up? Do you let them in or keep them out? Do you have friends who will be there for you should you need some help? Or do you have friends who are just there to take advantage of you? How do you let people treat you? Do they listen to you? Do they value what you say? Or do they ignore you constantly but still expect you to help them pick up the pieces when they have a problem?

A great quote from Tony Gaskins is, "You teach people how to treat you by what you allow, what you stop, and what you reinforce." Think about that. It's just like training a dog. If you don't want the dog to jump on you when you get home, you stop it from doing so and reinforce the correct behavior of sitting down before you pet him. You teach him how you want to be treated. Maybe it's time to step up in your life and let those around you know how you want to be treated.

It took me awhile to get this right and I hurt some feelings while I was getting better at it but I made it through and still held onto these important relationships. I was very angry and resentful because I had let myself be treated badly for a very long time. When I was done doing that, I found it difficult to politely ask to be treated differently. In retrospect, I would have prepared myself by getting heart-centered before embarking on any conversation where I was asking to be treated differently but I didn't know then what I know now.

Getting heart-centered prevents getting angry and resentful towards the person you are asking to change. A good way to have this conversation is to say something like, "It really hurts my feelings when you talk over me or interrupt me when I am sharing my opinion with you." Wait for a response. Don't fill in with more explanations. Let that simple statement sink in and if that person loves you, they will hopefully make a concerted effort to not do that again. When you first start out setting boundaries, you may be using this type of statement frequently. This is a great way to phrase it because it starts with your feelings and clearly states what is bothering you. Be sure to be heart-centered so it doesn't come across as angry or resentful or full of blame. If your request is tainted with anger or blame, the other person will **not** hear what you are saying. Did you catch that? If you want people to listen and truly hear you and begin to change how they treat you, you have to be heart-centered, almost neutral. That is the best advice I can give you.

You can even go so far as to say, "You know I should have told you this a long time ago and I'm sorry about that but it hurts my feelings when you don't greet me with a hug and a kiss when I get home each day." It may be that you've been living with something for years and yet you can still let someone you love know that something bothers you. It's OK. We all grow and change and we need to be accepting of this in ourselves and in others. Our needs may change over time as well and we need to be OK with that. And just as you are asking someone to treat you differently, you need to know that they can ask the same of you. By asking them to treat you differently, they may realize that they can do the same thing with you. You need to be open to that as well. Again, relationships are a two-way street. Be ready to change and accommodate their boundaries as well.

Boundaries can be set and reset as needed by us and by those we love. We let others know what is acceptable and not. If we don't let them know, they can't be expected to treat us the way we want to be treated. That's not fair. You can let them know gently and in a loving way.

My son has been very good at helping me practice my boundaries. Brené Brown, author of **Rising Strong**, defined boundaries as "what's OK and what's not OK." (Brown, Rising Strong, 2015) I had to teach my son how to treat me and let him know exactly what was OK and what wasn't. When he was around 11 or 12 years old, he tried on some behaviors that I didn't like. Sometimes he would walk away from me while I was correcting him about something, roll his eyes at me, mutter the terrible word, "Whatever" or continue looking at his smartphone instead of at me.

To me, this was unacceptable. I was not about to go through the rest of my life allowing him to treat me this way. I told him that this behavior was disrespectful and not allowed in our house. I explained that this is not how people in our family treat each other. I didn't do it to him and I expected the same in return. So every time he chose to display one of those behaviors, I had to call him on it. And I mean every time. I called him on it and gave him the consequence that he was well aware of. For example, if he was looking at his smartphone instead of at me during an intense discussion, he would lose the smartphone for the rest of the day.

That is called holding your boundary. And you know what? It works. My son is now 13 and rarely, if ever, displays one of those behaviors towards me (although I'm sure there are more behaviors to come as he moves further into his teenage years). I continue to teach him how to respect me and he still loves me. It's easier to do this in a parent/child relationship and more difficult with adults but it's still doable. Holding the line of how you want to be treated is so important. No one else will do this for you. It's completely up to you to let people know what is OK and what's not.

My son gives me plenty of opportunities to practice boundary setting and instead of seeing that as a bad thing, I'm actually grateful. This has helped me set boundaries in many other areas of my life and given me the courage to do it. What was a challenge in how to deal with my son became an opportunity to grow. Do you see that? Pretty cool, huh? I think our children can teach us so much if we are willing to learn. My son's constant pushing has helped me define and strengthen my personal boundaries and this has made me a better dolphin.

Setting boundaries creates respect for you as a person and this is especially important for parents out there. If you value yourself, others will too, even your kids. Plus, they learn to value themselves by watching your example. If you constantly cave to others' demands, what do you think your kids will do when they grow up? You want them to think for themselves and to stick up for themselves, right? Then you must start with the example of yourself and stand up to your own kids. Then they get a first row seat on how to start doing this for themselves.

Tell Tale Signs of Weak Boundaries

1. Resentment

If you find yourself feeling angry and resentful at random times towards the ones you love, then you may have weak boundaries. If you can't find forgiveness or compassion inside of you for even those you live with and love, then the problem might be weak boundaries on your part. Have you told the ones you love what your pet peeves are? Do you always pick up after everyone and then resent it? Do you do everyone's laundry because that's the way it's always been and resent it every time? Do you take the laundry to your loved one and practically throw it at them? It might be time to take a long, hard look at the things you do and how you feel about them. Does a change need to be made? Can you ask your loved one to do his or her own laundry? Take their dishes to the kitchen? Give you a hug and a kiss when he or she comes home? Say I love you? Ask how you are?

2. Gut Wrench

If your body is tense and your gut is tied up in knots, you may be suffering from weak boundaries. Are you saying yes to things you don't want to do? How does your stomach feel when you do this? Does your body feel relaxed? Just knowing that someone will ask you to do something you don't want to do, can make your gut wrench and your body go tight. Beginning to set boundaries eases this tension and lets you live in the present moment instead of dreading the next time so-and-so is going to ask you to do a favor for them. You won't avoid people because they might ask you to do something because you'll have gotten better and more comfortable with setting boundaries.

3. Angry Outbursts

I would often sit and take my son's disrespectful or bad behavior for several hours or even days and then when he did that one last thing that really ticked me off, I'd let him have it and yell at him. The outburst of yelling did not match the offense that I was yelling at him about. Do you understand that? For example, I might yell and scream and start crying because he wouldn't stop playing with the dog and put his dishes away. I'd be angry for hours and unable to look at him. He would be so confused and the afternoon would be an angry mess. My energy would drop super low and I'd be unable to do anything productive the rest of the day and judged myself as the worst mom ever.

My angry outburst was so unmatched to what my son did wrong because I let the wrong behaviors pile up and did not say anything. I DID NOT watch my boundary of what was OK so when my son crossed over my boundaries several times, I blew my top. This was bad for me and bad for him for so many reasons. Do you get that? If to begin with, I had calmly held my boundary for what was OK and reminded my son of this boundary or given him the consequence that matched the offense, I would have remained calm and centered. I would not have compounded the offenses and burst out in an overabundance of anger.

I remember early on in my relationship with my husband that I would keep track of his offenses in my head—ways that he had crossed over my boundaries. [Does this sound like something a shark would do? Absolutely.] These would fill my mind and I wouldn't say anything. I would seethe for days and then when he didn't unload the dishwasher or left a glass unwashed, I would go off. I would yell and cry and have a sudden outburst of emotion that did not match the situation. I was like a dam that had way too many leaks and was set to burst. I'm very glad my husband stuck it out with me. Now if I had calmly asked my husband to rectify each of those situations AS THEY HAPPENED in a heart-centered way, I would never have had the angry outbursts. Do you see how those are related? Life is just too short to keep a scorecard on your loved one's behavior. Instead, be the dolphin who shares what is OK and what is not OK when it happens. And just as important is listening to your loved one who shares his or her boundaries with you. Life is just better when you live this way. I know. I hardly ever have an angry outburst anymore and our home life is way more peaceful.

Summing Up

Setting boundaries may require some serious conversations with yourself and with your loved ones. You may need to start creating a space for you and those you love to share difficult things. This space needs to feel safe for all of you so you can share what is OK and what's not. And when you create this space, it can be a beautiful space for also sharing what you love about each other in deeper and more meaningful ways than you have allowed yourself before. These conversations, especially when they are difficult, lead to deeper connections and a more soul-satisfying life.

Here are a few more tips. In the course of setting up and strengthening your boundaries, you may find that some people don't value you. If this is the case, then maybe you need to rethink their place in your life or you may need to double your efforts to demand that your boundaries be kept in place. Stay strong and immovable in your request for each boundary. You may need a friend you can call and ask for support in holding your boundaries. Find another dolphin and explain what is going on. Maybe they can come with you to support you in a tough conversation or just be there to call or talk to afterwards. Dolphins like to help other dolphins so reach out. We are here to help each other, you know.

If you get good with holding your boundaries and only say "Yes" when you want to and it feels right, then you get an added bonus. Do you want to know what that bonus is? People will know you are a person of integrity and honesty. They know that when you say "Yes" or "No" that you mean it. They don't have to guess if you are saying "Yes" out of obligation or people pleasing efforts. They can relax in the knowing that you mean what you say and say what you mean. This allows for peace in relationships. There is no second-guessing. There is no fudging or not knowing what someone thinks. There is no resentment. There is no anger. There are just clean, clear relations. That is how dolphins interact in the world. Their intentions are clear. Their communication is transparent.

Everyone knows what they mean and you know what else? More people listen and listen more intently when you speak clearly and transparently with firm boundaries in place. They know you mean business and that you are not going to hit them over the head with a tangle of emotions or drama. You will speak your mind and share what your boundaries are and act accordingly. People know where they stand with you at all times because if you had a problem, you'd tell them straightaway. There is great comfort in that. People who want drama and second-guessing and bullying (like sharks and carp) may magically fall away from you as they recognize these new boundaries you have put in place and that, my friend, is a good thing.

Dolphins reap the rewards of respect, integrity of their word, and less drama by holding their boundaries clearly, transparently, and with love. Isn't that worth it? Value yourself and begin by setting small boundaries about what you want and how you want to be treated by others. You teach others how to treat you so start today.

Value Activity Worksheet

This can be done on an individual basis or as a family/couple. You can use the list of values below, create your own list, or add values to this list as you see fit. It's all about you and finding out what you value.

1. Make copies of this worksheet for each member of your family who can read and write.
2. Take 2-3 minutes and circle the values you think are the most important. Do this quickly and try to capture your first inclination. Try not to circle them all.
3. If you are in a group, take one person's sheet and put stars next to the values that show up on everyone else's list.

Integrity	Compassion	Honesty
Responsibility	Service	Fairness/Equality
Love	Balance	Gratitude
Courage	Humor	Respect
Loyalty	Patience	Self-Reliance
Trust	Cooperation	Helpfulness
Follow Your Heart	Awareness	Optimism
Resourcefulness	Stay in the Flow	Faith/Belief in Oneself
Confidence	Friendship	Acceptance
Humility	Oneness	Connection to Nature
Intuition	Mindfulness	Perseverance
Letting Go	Openness	Belief in Something Bigger than Self
Understanding	Belonging	Flexibility
Forgiveness	Generosity	Curiosity
Communication	Family Traditions	Family as Safe Haven
Kindness	Self-Control	

4. Choose and list the top ten values that were starred on the previous page.
5. You now have your top ten values as an individual or a family. Create a poster with all ten values on it and place it somewhere you or your family can see and refer to it daily.

_____
_____
_____
_____
_____
_____
_____
_____
_____
_____

Intentional Statement Activity

The intentional statement is like a mission statement for you as an individual or it can be a mission statement for your family. A business creates a mission statement to share the purpose of the company and its reason for existing. The mission statement also explains the goals and philosophies of the business. A family is even more important than a business and needs to be clear on its purpose, goals, and philosophies so the family can meet the needs of all of its members and provide a focus and centering point for the family.

1. List 3-4 adjectives that describe you as an individual or your family (examples—easy going, fun-loving, warm, kind, gracious, boisterous, quiet, etc.).

_____
_____
_____
_____
_____

2. List 3-4 values from your top ten list on the Value Activity Worksheet worked on in the previous assignment and write them here (examples—honesty, kindness, compassion, responsibility).

_____
_____
_____
_____
_____

3. List 3-4 goals you have as an individual or family in terms of being a better person or family. Examples might be "be more loving towards others," or "respect each other with words and actions" or "strive to be more responsible in our words and actions."

_____
_____
_____
_____
_____
_____
_____
_____

4. List 3-4 ways you want you or your family to show up in your community or in the world at large. Examples might be "environmentally responsible" or "considerate and friendly neighbors" or "contributing members of society."

_____
_____
_____
_____
_____
_____
_____
_____

5. Now take all the items from the previous action items and plug them in here to form your Intentional Statement.

"I am/The ____ family is (adjective #1), (adjective #2), (adjective #3), and (adjective #4). I/We believe in (value #1), (value #2), (value #3), and (value #4). My/Our goals is/are (goal #1), (goal #2), (goal #3), and (goal #4). I/We aim to be (community statement #1), (community statement #2), (community statement #3), and (community statement #4)."

EXAMPLE

"The Johnson Family is fun-loving, happy, caring, and sports-minded. We believe in cooperation, integrity, gratitude, respect, and forgiveness. Our goals are to respect one another, use gratitude to transition out of anger and frustration, balance family and school/work better, and to have more fun as a family. We aim to be kind and considerate neighbors, to volunteer and support organizations we believe in, and to be environmentally responsible citizens of the earth."

Your Intentional Statement:

_____
_____
_____
_____
_____
_____

6. Write the intentional statement clearly on a poster and place it where you and your family will see it daily. Rewrite it every six months or so to keep it fresh and relevant for where you are. A good time to do this is at the spring and fall equinox.

What I Love About Myself Activity

It's so important to love and value yourself. This is not selfishness or narcissism. This is recognizing you as a truly lovely human being who is walking on this planet right now and has a purpose for being here. Take five minutes and write as many things as you can that you love about yourself. Reach deep and be kind. For example, "I love that I can be kind and compassionate to others" or "I love my nose" or "I love my smile" or "I love how I set and maintain boundaries with my son." GO!

_____
_____
_____
_____
_____
_____
_____
_____
_____
_____
_____
_____
_____
_____
_____
_____
_____
_____
_____
_____

How I Want to Be Treated Activity

Are you clear on how you want others to treat you? Think about how you treat others. How would you like it if others treated you with the same depth of compassion, respect, and/or consideration as you show others? How would others treat you in your ideal world? How would you feel? Imagine and begin to write. This exercise helps you identify how you want others to treat you so just start writing and more will come. For example, "I want others to deeply listen to what I have to say" or "I want others to love me for who I am" or "I want others to love my silly, playful side" or "I want to be able to share things that are important to me and be heard."

_____
_____
_____
_____
_____
_____
_____
_____
_____
_____
_____
_____
_____
_____
_____

Family/Safe Space Meeting Guidelines

You can have meetings as a family or as a couple. You can call these meetings whatever you like. This is the kind of setting you want to create in order to share and redefine your boundaries. It is an excellent place in which to share what boundaries are and how they work to help us all get along with each other. Teaching our kids boundaries sets them up to be successful in their adult relationships. But even just having these meetings as a couple are crucial for maintaining peace and vitality between you.

Our family has meetings every couple of weeks or sometimes monthly or just when we need it depending on what is going on. But they are a part of how our family communicates and these meetings have become important to us. We use them to discuss what is working and what is not working in our family and household. We use them to discuss upcoming trips or holiday plans. And we use them to reconnect and share something we love about each other, which is one of the best parts.

How To Run A Family Meeting

1. Set up a time and place for a short 20 minute meeting where everyone is comfortable and can see each other (dining tables work well).
2. Let everyone know that no electronic devices are allowed at the meeting and no one is to answer the phone. This is family time. This lets everyone know that this time together is important—parents- don't go breaking this rule.
3. Inform everyone that there may be a list of several agenda items but that anyone can bring up a concern or idea at the end. This is an ideal place to discuss boundaries and ask if anyone wants to add boundaries to the agenda. Explain what they are and how they help us get along.

4. Bring a talking stick to the meeting. This can be a stuffed animal, pillow, a stone, or an actual stick. Its purpose is to let everyone know whose turn it is to speak. Remind other members about this if they speak out of turn or have them pass the talking stick on to that family member.
5. End each meeting with the "One Thing I Love About You" exercise. Each person must share one thing they love about each and every family member and go around the circle until everyone has done it. Use the talking stick to take turns. (Example: This would mean a young boy in a family of four would share one thing he loves about his sister, mother, and father. He would say "One thing I love about my sister is that I like to her hear play the violin. One thing I love about my Mom are her hugs. One thing I love about Dad is how he makes me laugh.")

Family Meeting Rules

1. To speak, you must have the talking stick.
2. Everyone is to be heard and listened to. This is a safe place for family members to speak their mind. Critical remarks, sarcasm, or making fun of others is not tolerated at a family meeting. Create a consequence if this behavior creeps up and make all family members aware of it. (Example: If you are caught criticizing, you have to do the dishes that night.)
3. No electronic devices allowed at any time. No phone calls. No texting. This means you parents!
4. Any concerns brought up during the meeting will receive respect and thoughtful consideration by all family members. If you can't think of a solution to the problem, table it, think on it, and address it later.
5. Make this a safe and happy time for your family by being loving and respectful at all times. If this means you must close your mouth and refrain from talking, do it.
6. Everyone must participate in the "One Thing I Love About You" exercise.
7. Anyone can call a family meeting even the youngest, smallest member of the family.
8. When someone calls a family meeting, a parent must evaluate if it's an appropriate time and place and see if all members can attend. If not, then a future time and place will be set for the meeting.
9. Recognize that your family is a team that works together and laughs together as well as lives together. Each person is important and needs to support everyone else.

Family Meeting Topics

1. You can have a family meeting about anything—an upcoming vacation, the start of school, general check-in, etc. If you don't know what to discuss, here are some ideas:
2. Buy a deck of **Table Topics** cards (Family Edition: http://www.tabletopics.com/Family-Edition-Cube) and use that to get the conversation started.
3. If you plan a vacation every year, include the entire family in the research and voting process (if that's OK) on where to go and what to do.
4. Do a general check-in with each member of the family to see if they have any issues or concerns they need to discuss.
5. About 2-3 weeks into a new school year, do a general review of how school is going. Ask which teacher is their favorite and what class they like the best or the least.
6. If you celebrate the holidays, you can discuss upcoming plans or research possible ways to be of service together during the holidays.
7. About a month before summer vacation, have a discussion on plans and activities for the summer.

Remember this is a sacred place to communicate. If something comes up that makes you angry, you can hit the pause button and restart the meeting at a later time. This is a safe place for your kids to communicate—give them the space to do that. AND starting this routine when they are young will make it much easier to have conversations about teenage issues when they are older.

[8]

PRACTICE GRATITUDE & IDENTIFY BEAUTY

"Gratitude is the fairest blossom which springs from the soul."
-Henry Ward Beecher

WHEN I WAS GROWING up, my mother had a bumper sticker that said, "Seek the good and praise it." I don't think I ever really got the deeper meaning of that. I grew up with positive New Age philosophy and knew that I felt better when I was positive. But it wasn't until I started a deep gratitude practice that I realized how important that saying was. It's basically saying to look around at your life, find what's good, and give thanks for it.

What we focus on expands. So if you want more good in your life, focus on what is already good and acknowledge it. This tells the universe that you would like some more of that good stuff please. This "attitude of gratitude" as some call it has been an important part of my daily happiness. I look around and quite literally can make myself cry tears of gratitude at how great my life is. That doesn't mean that everything is perfect. Being grateful is not about having life be perfect. It's about recognizing the good and being grateful for it despite everything that is going on. I'm so grateful and feel it so deeply in my heart on a regular basis that it shifts the energy around me faster than lightning. If you want one practice that will make you happier, this is it. It's the dolphin's secret to happiness, no matter the life circumstance of that dolphin.

Practicing gratitude daily is like building up muscles meaning that you get better at it the more you do it. Repetition is key. Take time throughout your day to notice what is going well and what is good. If you are having a terrible, yucky day, look out the window and be thankful the sun is shining. Be thankful you had hot running water for your shower. Be thankful you had food in your fridge so you could eat this morning. Be thankful there weren't bombs going off on your way to work or school. Be thankful you slept in a comfortable bed in a safe neighborhood. Start listing all of these things that you can start appreciating. There are many in the world who do not have these things including safe drinking water or dependable electricity. We have much to be thankful for. Tuning into that can reset our energy quickly. Once you start practicing this and list 10 to 20 things you are grateful for and feel deeply into that thankfulness, how do you feel? Do you feel calmer, more balanced? How does your outlook on the rest of you day look different than it did before?

Ways I use gratitude:
- To turn my crankiness around and get back to my heart-centered self.
- To go to sleep each night.
- To wake up each morning.
- To monitor myself to see if I need a time out to meditate (if I can't find anything to be grateful for in my current situation, then I take a time out).

The dolphins understand the preciousness of practicing gratitude every day and many times throughout the day. Whenever life comes up in a big wave of crisis or emotion, gratitude saves the day. It's like gratitude is your surfboard on the waves of life. Hold on to it for dear life and it will save you every time. Gratitude saves you from feeling bereft, lost, angry, jealous, or sad for too long. Don't get me wrong. Sometimes we need to feel all of those emotions, as they are a part of being human. But if you want to move out of feeling angry or upset, gratitude can get you on the next wave to somewhere else.

In our busy life, it can be way too easy to dismiss all the stuff and relationships and situations in which we find ourselves as just normal. It's not fair to do that. If we just slow down for a minute, we can recognize and be thankful for just how good we do have it. Did you have breakfast? Did you sleep on a bed? Do you feel safe most of the time going to work or school or home? Do you worry about where your next meal is coming from? Do you see the beautiful trees and flowers or hear the birds singing outside your window? Do you have people who love and care about you? How lucky are you, really? How many people in the world don't have these things or people or environment around them? We complain because we can't find an outlet to charge our smart phone or the line was too long to get our latte that morning while someone else starves or fears being bombed on their way to school or can't sleep at night due to the crime outside their window. Have you thought about that? That is part of being grateful.

Gratitude brings a certain grace to the dolphin. You see, dolphins know a secret. They know that giving thanks for what is good in their life brings them more good. Acknowledging the good in one's life tells the universe you like that and you want more of it. What we place our attention on is like a magnet for more of the same. If you spend your day complaining about what you don't like in your life, you are attracting more of the same. Is that what you really want? Turn that around. Begin to give thanks for the good things you already have in your life. If you believe there is not much to be thankful for, start small. Give thanks that you opened your eyes this morning. Give thanks for the breath you just took. Give thanks for standing on your feet. Give thanks that your arms work so you can brush your teeth. Give thanks for toothpaste and the feeling you have after you brush your teeth. Give thanks for the hot water you shower with. Give thanks for the food you eat and the water you drink. This level of gratitude starts you off fresh with a renewed appreciation of the world we live in. It brings you back to basics.

There is a leveling of life with a gratitude practice. Giving thanks brings you back to who you are—your authentic self. It reminds me of a thirsty child who is so happy to find a drinking fountain. The child beams with pleasure at the cool taste of the water from the fountain giving thanks for each mouthful. That attitude will bring you happiness during your darkest, most trying times. When in doubt, give thanks. When in fear, give thanks. When angry, give thanks. It shifts everything. It shifts your energy, your demeanor, and your current view of the world in a simple sentence of "I am grateful for...."

Others have taken this practice further and kept gratitude journals. A friend of mine kept a gratitude journal for a year and said it really changed his life. Something about having to remember throughout the day what you are grateful for and write it down before going to bed made him more aware and conscious of just what he was grateful for in his life. I recommend this if you feel so called to do it. I believe there are even some ready-made gratitude journals you can purchase to help you with this practice. It will turn things around for you and move you more towards the flow of living like a dolphin.

As a result of practicing gratitude, many experience a renewed awe and appreciation of beauty. I know because this happened to me. As I began to give thanks for what I saw and experienced around me, I became acutely aware of how beautiful it is when the sunlight comes down through the leaves or how amazing a rose can smell. I saw the beauty in the shrubs and palm trees on my street. I listened to the various songs of the mockingbird and the shrill cry of the red tailed hawk with new appreciation. I found beauty everywhere. I was amazed at how much beauty was around me. I found beauty in the sound of my son's laughter or the contented grunt of my dog after a good meal. I found beauty in the sounds of a busy city and the view from my patio. I found beauty in a quiet moment with my husband and in my own ability to snort when I laugh really hard. It is all beautiful. My life with all of its ups and downs is really a masterpiece of beauty. I appreciate all of it. With no dark, there would be no light. It is all yin and yang and beautiful in its yin and yang-ness. Practice this appreciation of beauty and sing the song of gratitude and you just can't be sad or angry for long. You will feel the pull to return to your natural state of gladness, quickly and easily.

Ways to Practice

1. Start a gratitude journal. Keep it for at least 30 days (or go for 365 days).
2. Write a sticky note that says "Gratitude" and put it next to your bed to remind you to think about what you are grateful before you go to sleep and when you wake up.
3. Spend five minutes each morning listing what you are grateful for (good to do while you are doing your make-up or in the shower or fixing kids' lunches).
4. Before going to bed each night, ask your child or spouse what event, person, or situation he or she is grateful for. It's a nice way to say good night and it helps everyone have good dreams.
5. Take the 10-Day Beauty Challenge where you take a picture (at least one) or video of beauty each day. Share the result with your loved ones.
6. Take a walk in nature and find 10 things that represent beauty to you. Enjoy it.

[9]

ENGAGE INTUITION & INTENTION

ONE OF THE DOLPHIN'S most important practices is engaging intuition and the power of intention. These two are so powerful and work so well together that dolphins cannot be stopped when they engage them at the same time.

Intuition is the practice of listening to that still small voice that you hear sometimes when you are quiet enough or receptive enough. Intuition comes from a place deeper and higher than your conscious awareness, if that makes sense. Some say it comes from your higher self. Some say it comes from angels and spirit guides who are here to help you. Some say it comes from universal source or the Force. I leave that up to you. It's only important that while heart-centered, you engage it and begin to practice listening to it.

So, how do you listen? Simple. Get quiet every day for a few minutes. If you meditate already, then it's simple to start tuning in and asking questions of your intuition. If you are not used to meditating, close your eyes in a quiet place where you won't get interrupted, put your hands over your heart, and breathe (just like in the mindfulness practice). Get yourself centered. Then you can ask yes or no questions of your intuition. Make sure you leave space and time for the answer to come and it shouldn't be an answer you think about or dissect in your head. The answer should just be there waiting for you. Beware though. Your ego is the voice that is shouting over and over and your intuition speaks softly and just once. Part of the intuitive practice is discerning the difference between these two.

Start by asking questions while in a relaxed, meditative state. Is it in my highest and best good to go to this party tonight? Wait for an answer—a clear answer. Should I call my best friend right now? Should I take the 805 freeway home? Yes or no questions are a good place to start and in your mind's eye (if you are a visual person), you can even invent a green light for yes and a STOP sign/red light for no. If there is more light around the STOP sign, then that's a no response from your intuition. If there is more light or the green light is really bright, then that's a yes response from your intuition. Does that make sense? A good imagination does help with this practice.

For example, you can use some other symbology in your mind's eye. Maybe you like to see a person you love holding up signs that say YES or NO or a big gong type object with YES on one side and NO on the other that spins and then lands on one or the other. Be creative. It's your intuitive practice and it should be fun and easy and clear.

The next step is to record your intuitive insights for 14-30 days so you can see how your intuition is doing over time. Start an **Intuition Journal**. Write down your question, the intuitive answer you receive, and then what you did as a result or the outcome. Your intuition told you to go to the party and you did and you had a great time. Or your intuition told you NOT to take the 805 freeway home but you did anyway and it took you an extra hour to get home. If you had gone on the other freeway, you would have made it home sooner. You can certainly ignore your intuition and see what happens with the outcome. That is kind of fun if you are using low risk, low gain questions to start with. See what happens. Play with it. Pretend you are a scientist with a hypothesis about your intuition and truly test it. Experiment. Just make sure you are heart-centered when you ask and listen well.

Don't listen to the voice of your loud ego but wait for that second, quieter voice that may or may not tell you what you want to hear. That quiet voice may tell you not to go to that party for some reason or another. It's up to you as to whether you follow the advice or not but do record the outcome. It's a great exercise that gives you confidence and acknowledges the power of your intuition. Every time you acknowledge your intuition and thank the universe for it, it grows stronger. The intuitive voice gets louder and it's easier to listen and quickly move forward. I know because I've done it and it works. Now I rely on my intuition for everything. Keep practicing and acknowledge it when it's right. We are all intuitive. And it is essential that we all start getting the hang of this. The world will be a better place if we do.

Intention

The other part of this important practice is the power of intention. I was raised believing that our thoughts create our reality. And over the years, I've sought out more and more spiritual teachers and they all say this same thing. One of my favorites is Mike Dooley who always signs his Notes to the Universe emails with "Thoughts are things so choose the good ones." (Dooley, 2011) What I didn't know until recently is that science is catching up to spirituality in beautiful ways. I loved **The Da Vinci Code** by Dan Brown when that came out a long time ago so it was not a hard decision for me to buy another of his books, **The Lost Symbol**, when that came out in 2009. That book set me on a new adventure of reading about quantum mechanics and quantum physics. One of the main characters, Katherine Solomon, who does research in this area, fascinated me. It turns out that her character was in part based on Lynne McTaggart and her work with **The Intention Experiment** (who I quoted several times so far in this book). (McTaggart, The Intention Experiment, 2007) I bought her book next and read it with underlines and sticky notes everywhere. I was fascinated. The power of intention was being proven in the world of quarks and quantum particles. It floored me. I went on to read several more of her books and although I am definitely no expert, I have enjoyed the dazzling repercussions of such research on the power of intention.

I got so excited about this topic that I gave a speech at my Toastmasters Meeting called "Quantum Mechanics, the Power of Intention, and Jell-O" based upon Ms. McTaggart's work in this area. Basically, it went like this. I started by describing four important things about quantum mechanics that I discovered by reading Lynne McTaggart's **The Intention Experiment**. I am paraphrasing the introduction from that book here as best as I understand it. The first was that atoms behave like messy, tiny clouds of probability. Every subatomic particle is not a stable thing. What I found fascinating was that atoms exist as a potential of any one of its future selves as if the atom is standing in a hall of mirrors staring at himself and all his possible selves. McTaggart describes reality at the quantum level as unset Jell-O. (McTaggart, The Intention Experiment, 2007) Have you ever made Jell-O? It's just liquid waiting to be put into a container until it sets and then it will hold that shape. This is what matter is at its smallest level—unset Jell-O.

Now we need to visit the work of Einstein. He discovered something he called "spooky action at a distance" or what others call entanglement which (from what I can understand) is when two particles that have been together and are then separated, react as if they are right next to each other. So you take two particles that have been together and then take one of them and put it in another room. Now if you change the magnetic orientation of the particle in this room, the particle in the next room will also change its magnetic orientation, as if it is still right next to the particle in this room. That is spooky.

The third thing I found interesting from McTaggart's book was that at this subatomic level, matter consists of little packets of energy constantly trading back and forth like passes in a basketball game. They are just transferring energy back and forth. This is why understanding your own energy is so important. And lastly, the most amazing thing discovered in this research was that the unset Jell-O only takes solid form and is measurable *when an observer was introduced*. It was only when the scientist decided to take a measurement of the subatomic particle that the matter or Jell-O chose a mold and settled into it. (McTaggart, The Intention Experiment, 2007) With these things in mind, can you not say that there is much more going on here than we previously thought or even imagined? Tiny particles of energy or matter are affecting one another in unexpected ways. These particles of matter connect and are in relationship with each other all the time. And in addition to that, these particles of matter are also in relationship with the observer. Now that's interesting. If we continue to follow that trail of breadcrumbs, what are the implications of this?

Well, the big A-HA here is that the moment we looked at an electron or took a measurement, it appeared that we helped to determine its final state. The observer affected the final state of the tiny particle. Did you get that? Read that sentence again. Our living consciousness, by observing and/or measuring the matter, somehow influenced the final state of the Jell-O. This may mean that reality is not fixed but is actually open to influence. Reality is open to our influence. Hmmmm. The implications of this are huge.

According to McTaggart's books (she's written several on the topic), a small group of scientists have been exploring these theories and testing them thoroughly with amazing results. (McTaggart, The Intention Experiment, 2007) If it's true that the act of observation or attention affects physical matter, then what is the effect of intention upon it? What if the observer doesn't just observe but deliberately tries to influence the final state of the physical matter? What happens then? What if we get to choose the shape of the Jell-O mold? What if that is up to us?

If the basic building blocks of our universe, like subatomic particles, can be influenced by the observer, then we need to ask ourselves how are we influencing the physical matter around us right now? How are we using our thoughts and our intentions in our daily lives? Are we even aware of this power within us? I bring you back to the quote from Mike Dooley, "Thoughts are things so choose the good ones." What if these thoughts truly are creating the reality of our lives? Wouldn't you want to choose the good ones? How would you go about doing such a thing?

I have experimented with intention in my own life and have found it to be a powerful tool. Did I say powerful? Yes, it's extremely powerful. The only way you'll believe me is to try it for yourself so I encourage you to do that. Be your own scientist. Test away. Experiment with your thoughts and intentions and see what happens.

For me, setting intentions tells the universe what you want to have happen in your life. You are setting up the Jell-O mold for the matter of your life when you set an intention. It creates your life for you. It's magical. It's amazing. It's a practice I do every day and it has worked miracles in my life. Every day, usually in the shower, I set my intentions for the day. I have two ways I work with intentions. I either use one in the original form as in, "It is my intention to live this day with focus and joy." (That was this morning's intention.) Or I treat the intention as if it is already coming true and I find this also very powerful. For example, every morning I say "Thank you for keeping me and my family safe, happy, healthy, protected, strong, and abundant. Thank you helping me move through my day with grace, joy, ease, flow, and love." I am giving thanks in advance. Once

I have set the intention, I let it go. That's a huge step. Then I know it will happen and expect it.

How to Set an Intention

1. Think of the intention you want to set and place it in a positive, gratitude format—"Thank you for..." or choose the format, "It is my intention to..."
2. Say it out loud or at least several times in your mind. Feel into it as much as you can. See yourself, after the event or activity you are setting intention for, feeling the way you want to feel. Think of what you will say or how people will look or what they will say. What emotions will you feel as a result of this intention coming true?
3. Finally, LET IT GO. Yes, let it go and trust that the universe is unfolding exactly as it should for your best and highest good.

So, let me give you an example. There is a couple we go out to dinner with sometimes and the woman is very picky about the food and the service and it has been unpleasant to dine with her in the past. We were on our way to their house to pick them up to go out to dinner and I was dreading the encounter because I didn't know what kind of mood she would be in. I decided to take action and set an intention. It couldn't hurt, right? I thought to myself, "Thank you for helping this dinner to be fun, pleasant, and delicious. Thank you for helping Betty to love the food, the service, and the whole experience." I pictured her in my mind's eye remarking on how good the food was and smiling and having a good time. I pictured myself at the end of the evening saying to myself, "Wow. That was fun. I had a good time." And then I let it go.

We arrived to pick up the couple and I lost myself in conversation and getting us to the restaurant on time. It wasn't until Betty remarked upon how good the food was that I remember I had set that intention before we left. I was dumbfounded and quite happy with the results of my experiment. I continued to do that every time we went out and it worked. If no one sets an intention for the evening like I did, then the Jell-O mold for the shapeless unset Jell-O just takes whatever shape it wants. If you want to reclaim power over how events happen in your life, start setting an intention for the Jell-O mold to flow into and see what happens.

Setting an Energetic Intention

In the first part of this book, I told you about the four different types of energy. They were personal, group or situational, foundational, and universal energy. I explained how Disneyland used their mission statement (being the happiest place on earth) as an intention to help set the foundational energy for each of their theme parks. You can do this too. You can set an intention for your home, your family (with their participation), your job, your community (again with community participation), and so on. You can set foundational energy by setting an intention and then posting that intention in that location so you see it every day and offer energy to it and visualize it until it is in place.

For example, you are a policewoman in a particular area of town. Before your shift, you can meditate to get heart-centered and then set an intention for your day something like, "Thank you for keeping this part of town peaceful, for keeping me and my partner safe and protected at all times, and for keeping all my constituents safe, happy, healthy, and protected. Thank you for giving me the intuitive guidance I need to make good decisions today that contribute to my highest good and the highest good of the people I serve. Thank you for helping me to keep the peace today." That is very powerful. Can you feel it? What if every police officer went around with that printed out on their dashboard? That sets a very strong foundational energy for the woman who is doing this job. Whether you're a teacher, doctor, dentist, yoga teacher, dog walker, or whatever, you can create a set of intentions that will set your day up for success.

Another example might be your own family. We went through a values exercise I created and completed an intentional statement for our family. It was fun and rooted the energy of our family in an intention. Currently, our family's intentional statement is this: "Thank you for helping the Pajak family to be fun-loving, sports-minded, happy, and curious. Thank you for helping us to live with more love, humor, integrity, and intuition. Thank you for helping us to be more active, travel more, listen to each other better, and have more fun as a family." Again, this is a powerful statement of who we want to be and sets the intention for how we want to show up in the world as a family. You can create intentions for every day uses or for family structures or for events or even for relationships. It just clarifies the energy you want that to have in your life so the universe can deliver.

Living Intention and Intuition

You've read a bit about intuition and a bit about intention. With this in mind, let me tell you another story involving intuition **and** intention both so you can see how I use these two tools together. Last fall, I set the intention for my day in the shower (my usual practice). Like I said before it usually runs along the lines of "Thank you for keeping me and my family safe, happy, healthy, protected, strong, and abundant. Thank you helping me move through my day with grace, joy, ease, flow, and love. It is my intention to live this day with joy and laughter."

I add in other things if people I know need some healing or light or love or if I want to move through the day with the energy of love or if I need extra good timing that day or whatever. I change it for what moves me. But generally, my days flow well with this kind of intention.

So, with that intention set, I went about my day. I had some errands to run including a trip to the grocery store. Every time I am in a grocery store, I have learned to listen to my intuition. I think the everyday use of our intuition is largely underutilized. Anyway, I perused the aisles and picked up what I needed but kept an ear out for the soft, still voice inside that is my intuition in case it wanted to pop up and have me get something.

I'm going down the sundries aisle and my intuition called out to me to stop and buy the Aloe Vera Gel. I looked at the Aloe Vera Gel and my logic and reasoning kicked in protesting the purchase. It's not even summer anymore—what use would you have for Aloe Vera Gel? No one was going to get sunburned. I looked at the price. It was only $2.79 so I weighed my logic versus my intuition. I know my intuition is right 99% of the time so I decided to purchase the Aloe Vera Gel. Heck, it was only $2.79. I went with the flow there and continued on with my day still not understanding the reasoning behind the purchase but I was willing to play it out and see how it would unfold.

The next day, I am replacing a doorbell on the apartment at our rental property that I manage. (I shared some of this story earlier in this book.) It had been awhile since I'd done any handyman type of work but I pulled out the power drill that you can use as a screwdriver to work on the doorbell. In less than ten seconds, I stripped the screw and bent it sideways using the power drill. Smoke came off the drill and I stopped. Oops. Without thinking, I reached out with my pointer finger towards the screw I had just stripped to touch it. OUCH! Oh my gosh. How stupid. The screw was burning hot from the power drill. What was I thinking? I looked down at my pointer finger and there was a lovely circular imprint of the top of the screw burned into the pad of my finger like a bad tattoo. It burned like crazy. In that moment, I was sure that I would need to amputate the entire top of my finger—it hurt that bad. I ran some cold water over it for a few minutes...until...I remembered...that the best thing you can put on a burn like this is Aloe Vera Gel. And I had just bought some.

This is totally how my life works. This is what I call living in the flow. I seem to have whatever I need at my fingertips (literally) when I need it if I set intention and follow my intuition. The flow follows behind that naturally. How did I know that I would need that Aloe Vera Gel the next day? I think that is pretty cool. I like living in the flow like that. Generally, it makes things work so much more smoothly.

However, I am still working on my intuition. For example, I wish my intuition had told me not to strip that screw on the doorbell in the first place so I wouldn't need the Aloe Vera Gel at all. Ha! Ha! But aren't we all a work in progress? Actually, it wouldn't have happened at all if I had stayed mindful and heart-centered in the work I was doing. So there you go.

Just to reiterate, Lynne McTaggart shared that, "Intention appears to be something akin to a tuning fork, causing the tuning forks of other things in the universe to resonate at the same frequency." (McTaggart, The Intention Experiment, 2007) I believe intention is a tuning fork calling to you that desire you put out into the universe. If you take my example of setting an intention about having a pleasant dinner, it's almost as if the intention for the dinner is chaotic or just soft if no one sets out to create an intention about that dinner. So it's left to whatever happens at that dinner table to direct and guide the evening. But if I set an intention to have it be a great dinner where everyone is satisfied with their food and the conversation is light and enjoyable, the tuning fork goes into effect calling that experience forward through the universe. It's powerful and it's exciting.

Pitfalls of Intention Setting

But what happens if your intention fails? What has happened if your intention did not work? That is a good question. If your intention fails, look back at your intention. Was it too specific? Did you set intention for another human being to do something? Did you set your intention to win the lottery? Each one of those intentions contains pitfalls. First, you can be too specific with an intention. Let me give you an example.

It was time for us to get a new car. I was tired of my used mini-van and I was convinced that everyone on the road did not want to drive behind a mini-van and they all zoomed around me. Anyway, my husband and I started looking at cars and we were convinced we wanted a brand new Toyota Highlander. I set an intention something like, "Thank you for a brand new Toyota Highlander for our family" and I had envisioned me happily driving around in a new car. They looked awesome and got high ratings for safety and reliability. It would fit all of our stuff and our dogs.

It was a Friday and I told my husband I had cleaned out the mini-van and it was ready to take for a trade-in at the Toyota dealer on Saturday. My husband started looking at dealers and how much a Highlander cost. After my son went to bed, my husband sat me down and we looked at the price together. At that moment, we realized that we could not afford a brand new Highlander. Oh man, I was crushed. Why we had not looked at prices before, I don't know. But when we did, I was so sad.

I had set intentions around getting a Toyota Highlander and I couldn't believe that now we were here, it wasn't going to work. This intention setting stuff was bull. I went into my home office and cried. I was so upset. How could this be? About an hour later, my husband printed something on the printer and came in to get it. He told me he found something else in our price range that I might like. I couldn't even look at it that night. The next morning (after the sleep reset my energy levels), I looked over the printout and saw a rather nice Toyota RAV4 that was a few years old but in great condition. It was a golden-beige, which was not a color I had thought of before, but it looked nice. I checked in with my intuition and got a yes on checking it out. I had a funny excited feeling in my belly. Maybe this was the car I saw in my vision? And this one we could afford. We drove to the dealer and ended up making a deal and trading in the old mini-van for that golden RAV4. I was over the moon with our "new" car and still happily drive that car today.

But do you see what I did wrong in my intention setting? I was way too specific in some ways and not specific in others. My intention was "Thank you for a brand new Toyota Highlander for our family." A better intention might have been, "Thank you for a safe, reliable car that fits our needs, looks and drives great, is in great condition, and is affordable that we will love for years to come." Does that sound a little better?

You see when you create a more open-ended intention that is still specific, it allows the universe to serve it up to you in more creative ways. There are a lot more possibilities available in that second intention allowing for the intention to work more quickly while also being more tailored to your specific needs. Mike Dooley in his book, **Leveraging the Universe**, discusses the "cursed hows" where people set the vision of exactly how that intention is going to show up in their lives but this is a mistake, as seen in my example of the Highlander. Dooley writes, "But when we understand the truth behind all manifestations, we can start initiating change from the inside out, beginning with a vision and then physically showing up to be availed of life's magic, leaving the actual hows to divine intelligence." (Dooley, 2011, p. 15)

Be sure to set intention for what you really want but don't start writing in **how** it will manifest in your life. Don't envision how it will manifest either. That will be too limiting. For example, don't envision buying that car from a particular dealer or on a certain day. Let the universe line that up for you. Trust me, the universe will do a much better job. It can line things up way more magically than we can imagine just like it did with my RAV4. I think my husband had a better vision and intention for buying a car as he magnetized that

RAV4 into his sphere of attention quickly and easily. I was stuck on details. That is one potential pitfall in intention setting.

Another common pitfall is setting an intention like, "Thank you for bringing Bob to me as my new boyfriend who will love and cherish me." That is nice but what if Bob is not your soul mate or is not particularly good for you at this moment in your life. A better intention might be, "Thank you for helping me allow a special someone to come into my life who I love deeply and who loves me deeply in return who I get along well with, laugh with, and want to share my life with for my best and highest good and the highest good of all concerned." That is more specific but does not name names.

You can't set intention around another person to do something you want them to do. Free will is a very real aspect of each individual's life. When you set that second intention, it frees up the universe to bring to you that special someone who is a perfect fit for you who may or may not be Bob. Get it? The same goes for setting intentions for other people. You can't direct other people's lives as much as you would like to. You can send love to other people in the form of intentional statements. One I use a lot is "Thank you for sending love, light, and healing to Patricia" if Patricia is having a rough time or a physical ailment. This works really well. You are sending packets of love energy to Patricia and that is a great thing and has been known to heal people. However, the setting of romantic intentions around a specific person will never work.

I get asked a lot if I have won the lottery because I am so good at setting intention and my intuition is very strong. Shouldn't I be able to pick the winning numbers and set the intention of winning lots of money? Apparently, everyone opening up to his or her intuition asks this question. First, let me ask you if you have ever researched the people who won the big lottery jackpots to see if they have achieved happiness in their life? You may be surprised to hear that lottery winners commit suicide or are murdered at a much higher rate than your regular every day person. They are much more likely to have problems with family and friends over the money and often spend it all ending up penniless. Happiness is not a part of their lives. As we've all been told, money does not equal happiness and these lottery winners are very real examples of that. Sure you need enough money so you have your basic needs such as housing, food, and clothing taken care of so you can even think about being happy. That's a given. After that, happiness becomes more of a daily choice.

But I think the more important thing here is that there is a trajectory to our life where having a lot of money may or may not help certain parts of our lives along. It is my belief that we set up some aspects of our life before we get here to learn certain things in the school of our earthly life. We set ourselves up for specific experiences. We want to stretch, strive, and grow while we are in earthly form and the circumstances of our life help us do this.

I know that if I had won the lottery last year, I would not be following through on writing this book which is something I feel very drawn to do. I am hopeful that in writing this book I can help others and be of service. If I was sitting in piles of money, I would not have the drive to sit down and work on this book and work on creating a career out of helping others understand what I've learned. I am pushed forward. I have perseverance and determination. Winning the lottery would rob me of that and it would rob me of the experience of writing this book (which I am enjoying tremendously). I am quite happy writing this book.

Hard conditions create opportunities to grow and find more of our authentic self and learn new ways to be in the world. So this is where the idea of drawing to us situations and experiences that are for our best and highest good comes in. Winning the lottery may not be in your best and highest good. You might miss out on some important opportunities to grow as a person that will help you find your soul mate and live a happier life. That is why I end each and every intentional statement with the phrase "for my best and highest good." This allows the universe to work its magic and calls on divine intelligence to help draw to you what will work best for you at this time. I also add "with grace and ease" because I'd rather move through this life a bit more gently if possible.

It also seems to me a much better goal for an intention is for happiness than for money. If you are happy, you should assume that your financial needs have been met, right? Plus, happiness is a much fuller experience of life than simply rich or well off? Money doesn't buy happiness. If you set your intention to be happy, the financial part of it will come and support you along with all the other things that make you happy—friends, lovers, satisfying work, comfortable housing, etc.

There is one last pitfall and that is not letting go of the outcome. If you set intention and never let it go, the universe can't work its magic. You are holding on too tightly. It's as if the universe needs to take your intention like an order at a restaurant and give it to the cook but you won't let go of it so nothing happens. Set the intention again, visualize it, and then let go. If you find yourself returning again and again to this intention in your mind, redirect your mind. Find a task or hobby that is all consuming to take your mind off of it. Get involved in a good book or a movie. You are in charge of your mind so redirect its attention elsewhere.

I especially have to do this when I set an intention to find a parking space. I have to let go for the parking space to appear. You get better at it with time and practice and then you start amazing yourself. I am the parking queen now. I've gotten very good at finding a parking space in a crowded city at lunchtime and usually it's a spot right in front of where I want to go.

Have fun practicing the art of setting intentions and using your intuition to follow through. This is the flow of the dolphin. It's how they sail through life with a smile on their face. They use the magic of the universe to create happiness for themselves and others. As Mike Dooley wrote, "You create your corner of the world and all that you experience." (Dooley, 2011, p. 19) So go have fun creating!

Intuition Practice

This is a place where you can begin practicing with your intuition. Ask a question about a mundane task or thing going on in your life. Write down the date and the question. Then center yourself per the mindfulness exercise at the beginning of this book (Stop—Observe—Reset with hands over your heart). Breathe. See in your mind's eye a Yes/No sign and think of the question. Then let an answer come to you. Don't force it. Write down the answer you got here. Then later, check back and write down what the outcome was. You'll get better with practice and start to recognize the difference between your ego and the still, small voice of your intuition.

Example:

Date	Question	Yes/No	Outcome
3/22	Should I go to Susan's party tonight?	Yes	It was a great party and I was more outgoing than I thought I could be. I met a nice guy too. He asked for my number.

Your Turn:

Date	Question	Yes/No	Outcome

Intention Activity

Start to practice setting intentions here. You may end up enjoying this practice and start an Intention Journal where you can watch your progress over time and see how many of your intentions have manifested. That is a lot of fun. You can set daily intentions, yearlong intentions, or intentions around specific topics. Have fun with it.

How to Set an Intention

1. Think of the intention you want to set and place it in the gratitude format—"Thank you for..."
2. Say it out loud or at least several times in your mind. Feel into it as much as you can. See yourself, after the event or activity you are setting intention for, feeling the way you want to feel. Think of what you will say or how people will look or what they will say. What emotions will you feel as a result of this intention coming true?
3. Finally, LET IT GO. Yes, let it go and trust that the universe is unfolding exactly as it should.

Daily Intention

Example: "Thank you for helping me live love every day in all my thoughts, words, and actions."

_____
_____
_____

Relationship Intention

_____
_____
_____

Career Intention

_____
_____
_____

Health and Wellness Intention

_____
_____
_____

Prosperity Intention

_____
_____
_____

Self-Cultivation Intention

_____
_____
_____

Friends and Family Intention

_____
_____
_____

[10]

LIVE IN FLOW & PLAY IN JOY

I BELIEVE FLOW IS so important to the life of a dolphin that I need to include two different types of flow in this section. One I was introduced to over twenty years ago but sort of forgot about. When my son was little he would get obsessed with some things and did them over and over and over. It used to annoy me to no end. Like learning to blow bubbles with bubblegum or learning to whistle. Again at age 6, he loved the challenge of learning to ride his bike with no training wheels. Now those challenges are things like getting better in soccer, learning Spanish, or learning new tricks on his kendama (a ball and cup toy that was popular for awhile). I could never figure out why he liked doing these things over and over and over again to get better at it until I recently came across this old book I read while at UCLA called **Flow: the Psychology of Optimal Experience** by Mihalyi Csikszentmihalyi.

It makes perfect sense now. The light bulb went on in my head. When my son was working on blowing a better bubble or learning to whistle, he was in a state of flow. When he was learning tricks on his kendama (similar to a yoyo), he was in a state of flow. The challenge was right at the place between boredom and anxiety and within his ability to reach it. He sought out activities like this all the time and now I totally understand.

Csikszentmihalyi wrote in his book, **Flow: The Psychology of Optimal Experience**, "Flow is the way people describe their state of mind when consciousness is harmoniously ordered, and they want to pursue whatever they are doing for its own sake. In reviewing some of the activities that consistently produce flow—such as sports, games, art, and hobbies—it becomes easier to understand what makes people happy." (Csikszentmihalyi, 1990)

But it's more than just playing baseball or painting a picture. Csikszentmihalyi explains that, "Enjoyment appears at the boundary between boredom and anxiety, when the challenges are just balanced with the person's capacity to act." (Csikszentmihalyi, 1990)

That is what I found interesting. A challenge can get you into the state of flow but it can't be too hard and it can't be too easy. I now realize one reason why my son is so happy. He enjoys a challenge. If you say something is hard to my son, then he says, "Really?" and gets excited to check it out.

I think as adults we forget how much fun can be had learning something new or taking on a challenge. We look forward to sitting in front of the TV after clearing the dishes, taking the dog for a walk, and making sure homework is done but you know what? That TV watching is not actually a "flow" activity.

In fact, Csikszentmihalyi shares that "...TV watching, the single most often pursued leisure activity in the United States today, leads to the flow condition very rarely. In fact, working people achieve the flow experience—deep concentration, high and balanced challenges and skills, a sense of control and satisfaction—about four times as often on their jobs, proportionately, as they do when they are watching television." (Csikszentmihalyi, 1990)

Now this was written in 1990 before the introduction of the Internet and the wide use of videogames and smartphones. I have to wonder if the rise in videogame use might be attributed to kids and adults both getting into a state of flow while playing. I think it's important to remember, though, that we can achieve a state of flow while doing other activities like sports, art, writing, making music, or playing board games as well.

Csikszentmihalyi continues with, "The best moments usually occur when a person's body or mind is stretched to its limits in a voluntary effort to accomplish something difficult and worthwhile. Optimal experience is thus something we make happen." (Csikszentmihalyi, 1990, p. 3)

So, how do you know if you are in a state of flow? These activities require the learning of skills, they set up goals, they provide feedback, and they make control possible. They allow the participant to achieve an ordered state of mind. Let me provide an example to make this clear. I went to a party last year where we had a Texas Hold 'Em Poker tournament and my husband and I decided to play. There were 14 adults in the tournament. I had previously learned how to play and had acquired the skills. The goal was to win as much fake money as possible by winning hands. You get immediate feedback after each hand as to whether or not you were gaining on your goal of winning money. You just needed to look at your stack of chips. I was in control of my moves of whether I want to check or raise a bet or fold my cards. And I was in an ordered state of mind. I was in the flow of it because time passed without me noticing. It also helps to be highly intuitive in the game of Texas Hold 'Em and that made it even more fun. I was in the final three before I realized we had to get home as it was late. This is what is means to be in a state of flow.

Can you think of activities where you have been in the state of flow? What were you doing? Did the activity require you to learn something or have knowledge of how to do it? Were there specific goals? Did you get feedback on how you were doing? When you were in it, did you lose track of time or forget to eat or not even think about going to the bathroom? Then you were in a state of flow.

What I find very interesting is that when I was doing research on mindfulness and sports, I came across a research study about teaching mindfulness to swimmers and golfers who attained better performance results and scattered throughout the study were citations from Mihalyi Csikszentmihalyi. (Bernier, Thienot, Codron, & Fournier, 2009) This study led me to another study by Y.H. Kee, C.K. John Wang, where they discovered "The findings suggest that those with the propensity to be more mindful are also more likely to experience the flow states." (Kee & Wang, 2008) Kee and Wang conclude that mindfulness and flow may be symbiotic and that developing mindfulness leads to flow experiences. This is something to consider if you want more flow experiences in your life.

In order to have happier moments and activities, we must be able to recognize what gets us into this state of flow. Then we can be sure to add those into our day or our weekends so we get more satisfaction out of life. It's really great when you can turn every day tasks or aspects of your career into flow activities. Then you are really set.

Some questions to ponder...
- What activities get you into the state of flow?
- What are you doing when you lose track of time or forget to eat?
- What activity challenges you? Is it playing a new videogame or helping your dog master a new trick or shooting hoops or solving a Rubik's cube?

Think about what you love to do. Is it an activity where you achieve a state of flow? Finding flow is a lifelong ingredient for living a happier and more contented life so this is an important thing to take note of.

That was the first definition of flow that I learned back in college but since then I've discovered another type of flow that is also important to the dolphin. And this one is very natural for dolphins. It is just how they live. They move effortlessly from one thing to the next with that little smile on their face because the flow brings them joy and joy brings them flow. These two are intertwined in this type of flow.

When you are practicing the tools of intuition and intention, you begin to experience flow of a different type. This is a way of moving through your day with grace and ease. You set your intention to move through your day with perfect flow and then you listen to your intuition as you move throughout your day to see what to do first or where to be or who to track down. If you follow the flow of your day, you will find synchronicity everywhere. This is different from the flow mentioned previously and I think both types are extremely important for the life of the dolphin.

One thing I always do is follow my intuition on what to do about lunch. Often I find I get a picture in my head of where I should eat lunch that day for my best and highest good. I'll follow that intuition and as I'm eating lunch, I'll realize that there is a shop selling that one item I couldn't find on my list right next door. Or I'll run into an old friend and get to say hello. I listen to the timing as well. Should I go now to lunch or finish this paragraph? The timing is just as important and I use that a lot now. I'll think to myself, should I do those errands after I pick up my son from school or do I have time to do them before? I'll hear that still small voice say to do them before I pick up my son and I find I have just enough time to complete them all. Then when I do pick up my son, I discover he's not feeling well and wants to go straight home. Good thing I did those errands before I picked him up. That is flow. That is living in the flow of life. It makes life so much better. I can't stress that enough. Living in the flow just brings relief and peace to your day.

It took me a long time to get to living in this flow state most days. It came along naturally as a result of setting intention and following my intuition. It was not something I had to work at but instead just listen to. Again, this comes back to mindfulness as well. I have to listen to my intuition and my body and my energy level. I'm always checking in as to what is the best path forward. Should I take a nap or carry on and get these few tasks done first? Should I go to the grocery store now or wait until lunchtime? There is a certainty and ease that comes when you practice this over and over and learn to ride the waves of your own energy and your own intention/intuition practices. It's very relaxing once you begin to trust this process.

And you know what? When you are feeling relieved and peaceful, you have greater access to joy on a daily basis. Things don't get stuck or out of whack or at least, much less often. They just move along and next thing you know, you are belting out Fleetwood Mac songs in your car laughing at yourself feeling joyful. OK. Maybe that's just me but it can happen when I am experiencing joy.

Sarah Ban Breathnach, author of **Simple Abundance**, wrote, "Learning to live in the present moment is part of the path to joy." (Breathnach, 1995) That is what flow is, living in the present moment, so of course, it leads to joy. That is how it works. Playing in joy means that you have achieved a state of flow. Think of real dolphins and how flowing and playfulness lead to the joy as they fly out of the water and do flips.

If you follow the joy, then that can lead you to flow. If you follow the flow, it can lead you to joy. They are two sides of the same coin. Does that make sense? It's like a river steadily moving downstream. You can fight it. Or you can laugh, jump in, and go for a ride. If you have set your intentions for a safe trip and use your intuition to guide you around the boulders in the river, you'll have a great time in flow and joy. That is how it works.

[11]

Practice Acceptance & Care of Self & Others

ACCEPTANCE IS THE OPPOSITE of judgment. I learned this from a very special teacher, Beatrex Quntanna, author of the **Moon Book**, who practically beat me over the head with this mantra for five years (which I am really grateful for, by the way). I'm still working on it but I get it now, more than ever. You see I lived as a carp for over thirty years. I lived every day in judgment of everyone else and especially myself. If you thought I was harsh and judgmental of others, you didn't hear how harsh I was internally within my self. Carps never think they are good enough so neither is anyone else. I can still fall into this pattern but it doesn't happen as often so I'm glad. I think I've made progress.

What started me down the road of acceptance and away from judgment was beginning to look at people I was judging as their eight-year-old selves. I began to picture them as children. This gave me access to compassion, forgiveness, and finally acceptance for who they are. I realized that we are all just trying to get along. We all want to be happy and feel loved. You don't know what trials that person has been through or what is going on with them. That person that cut you off in traffic might be on their way to see their loved one who is dying in the hospital. That person that yelled at the waitress for lousy service might have just been diagnosed with cancer earlier in the day. We don't know the roads that others have travelled on. We don't know what fears or experiences they face down every day just trying to move forward. There are addictions, abusive relationships, financial crises, health issues, and so on that we all face. Try to give this person the benefit of the doubt. Have a little compassion. If you were facing one of these terrible situations, you would want someone else to do the same for you. There is a famous quote that says, "Everyone you meet is fighting some battle you know nothing about. Be kind. Always." Let me share a story that sticks with me.

For various reasons, we put our son into a private school with a high tuition but we were only able to do this with the financial help of generous family members. We couldn't afford it on our own and I found myself very uncomfortable meeting the other parents because I prejudged them as all being so different from me. They all drove Teslas and Porsches and lived in the swanky part of San Diego. I figured they were just so rich that I'd have nothing in common with them. I held back from getting to know any other parents for two years. I just felt so different. I thought I wasn't good enough or dressed well enough and that my old Toyota RAV4 wasn't cool enough.

Then as I was sitting watching my son play flag football, I started talking with two moms and heard more of their story of how they grew up. I realized we had a lot more in common than I previously thought. In fact, their stories of working extremely hard to get through high school and working two jobs in college were nothing short of remarkable. They were both driven to get to a place where they could relax about money and they both did it. I admired them and walked away with a very different viewpoint about the other parents at my son's school which was a good thing. I feel much more relaxed about meeting other parents now and try to leave my judgmental self at home. You just never know what people's story might be. My idea that I wasn't good enough to hang out with these people was a fallacy. They may live in fancier homes than me but that doesn't matter. We're all just people with interesting stories of how we got to where we are. I learned something about myself that day.

Judgment creates separation from others and moving forward, I am choosing acceptance so I can create more connections. Other people can be our greatest source of wisdom if we are open to learning from them. I realized that because my life was easier growing up (financially stable with two parents who doted on me) that I was not as driven to make a lot of money. That was an interesting revelation about who I am and why I've lived my life the way I have.

WAYS TO AVOID JUDGMENT

1) View each person we meet as a teacher.

They have something they can teach you and if you approach each person from that point of view, you won't fall into judgment so easily.

Ralph Waldo Emerson wrote, "Shall I tell you the secret of the true scholar? It is this: Every man I meet is my master in some point, and in that I learn of him."

This allows for curiosity and acceptance to edge in before judgment. If you believe in synchronicity like I do, you can wonder why this person is now in your orbit? What do you have to learn from him or her? This is a great way to avoid judgment and move towards acceptance and yes, even those people that tick you off are teachers. They might be your best teachers so pay attention.

2) Remember the principle of oneness and the mirror effect.

If you have not heard this before then listen in. If you believe we are all one and that we are all drops of the one ocean (think connected to each other by the Force from Star Wars), then if I judge you, aren't I also judging myself? Why would I want to judge myself? Wouldn't

I rather accept myself exactly the way I am, imperfections and all? Wouldn't I rather everyone accept me just as I am? That's the first part.

The second part of the oneness principle is the mirror effect. What we notice or judge in others is actually reflecting back to us a part of ourselves that we may need to look at. If you see jealousy in someone else, is there a touch of jealousy somewhere in your own behavior? Maybe you need to look at that. What if you judge someone else as stupid or unaware or unwilling to listen? Is there something you need to look at in your own life around one of these criticisms? Is there a situation in your life where you are not listening or are unaware? I often find this is the case so I try to use my compulsion to judge someone as a way of reflecting on my own behavior to see if there is something that needs adjusting.

Then you can also ask if you need to accept this as part of yourself so that you can also accept it in others? Could recognizing a flaw in others help you be more accepting of flaws in yourself? Can you make that a part of how you move through life so that you move away from judgment and more towards acceptance?

3) Walk a mile in their shoes.

You don't know what other people have gone through and what trials they are enduring so don't judge them. The character of Atticus Finch from **To Kill A Mockingbird** put it best when he said, "You never really understand a person until you consider things from his point of view...until you climb into his skin and walk around in it." (Lee, 2015)

There are reasons people act the way they do, dress the way they do, and say the things they say. People who hurt inside do and say things that hurt others. You have not walked in their shoes and experienced what they have in their life so accept them as they are and help where you can. Judging does not help but a compliment, a kind word, or a smile, can help a lot.

If someone does something hurtful or rude to me like cutting me off in traffic or saying something awful, I try very hard to not judge him or her. Instead, I see them as the hurt little child that is inside of them and send them love. I get my own energy stable and I breathe and send love to them so that their day gets better. And then I let the situation go. At least, that's what I try to do on good days when I am feeling steady and balanced. I don't bring up the situation to every other friend I see that day because that just adds negativity to the world—to my world. I'd rather see what my friend is excited or happy about and share what is good with me than dwell on what a person who was hurting did to me.

4) Accept that people are doing their best.

Recently, I've had the pleasure of reading Brené Brown's book, **Rising Strong**. She writes in depth about a concept that a few years ago, I started using in my acceptance practice. She questions whether we can use the phrase that "people are just doing their best in that moment" and to cut them some slack. She asks many people whether or not they think that statement is true. I happen to agree with that statement. I do believe people are trying to do their best with what they've got in that moment and in believing that, I was able to release judgment and find acceptance. Ms. Brown describes her husband's answer about whether or not he believes that to be true and he says he's not sure but when he believes that people are doing their best, he is happier and more positive. I feel the same way. It's generous to think the best of those people around you and leads to a happier daily existence. (Brown, Rising Strong, 2015)

George Orwell summed it up this way: "Happiness can exist only in acceptance."

A few years ago, I had the opportunity to look back at something that happened during my life where I felt some people acted badly towards me. I began to think about that situation in a new way. I looked hard at the woman who had verbally attacked me and I began to think about her as a little girl. She had obviously learned how to relate to people by watching her parents. I realized in that moment how frightening her childhood must have been. One of her parents must have had a true knack for finding weaknesses and going for the jugular with a verbal attack. There was such viciousness in the attack I experienced that I knew this woman had been on the receiving end of many similar attacks. It was then that my heart changed. I went from blaming her to forgiving her. I went from anger to compassion. This woman was relating to people in the only way she knew how—like a shark. I'm sure she had been hurt many times just like she had wounded me.

I realized that she was doing the best she could with the tools and experiences she had had up to that point in her life. She was truly doing the best she could and with that new awareness, I came to a place of acceptance. And just so you know, I did all of this internal work without ever speaking or meeting her again. There was no need to actually see her to get to a point of acceptance. The situation was eased on my end and that was all that I required. I felt better about the whole situation way after it was over. But it was still important to do that internal work and let go of any residual anger because that was hurting me. Reaching a level of acceptance that she was doing the best she could gave me freedom from that situation ever hurting me again.

5) *Acceptance leads to freedom and flow.*

Acceptance helps us create a path to compassion for others and freedom for our self. If we aren't doing a very good job on something, maybe we need to say "Well, that's the best I can do right now and I'm going to be OK with that." That's actually very healthy. You are being accepting of what you can do and who you can be right then. It doesn't mean that you won't strive to do better. It just means that you can accept where you are and what you are being in that moment. That takes the stress off. That lets you move forward.

Remember that perfectionism is friends with judgment. You are judging that you are not good enough or that what you've created is not perfect. Let it go. Let it be good enough for that moment.

Judging yourself or others stops the flow. Let that sink in for a moment. How much joy do you feel when you are being judgmental? I mean true joy—heartfelt joy. It stops. So does your intuition. It all stops. When you feel acceptance in place of judgment, you are open. You are free. You can listen to your intuition. You can find the flow again.

6) Judgment leads to separation. Acceptance leads to connection.

Being judgmental separates you from others. Sometimes this is a method of self-defense that carp use. They judge others to keep distance between them and another person because if they reject them first, then they don't have their feelings hurt. But sharks also use judgment to keep the illusion in place that they are better and smarter than others. Remember, sharks always need to be better than others and use judgment as a shield to protect this belief.

When you fall into acceptance of others, you realize we are all human beings with our flaws and our strengths and this leads to a basis for connection. You can connect with someone you accept and others can connect with you once you accept yourself. Acceptance works to better your relationship with yourself and with others. Do you see how that works? Being human helps us come together. When we accept that we make mistakes and aren't perfect, that's when we connect. Think of all the characters in all the books and movies you've ever experienced. The ones we love the most are the characters that are full of flaws as well as strengths.

7) Judgment supports fear. Acceptance supports love.

Judgment brings fear. Judgment is based in fear. You fear that someone else will judge you as you have judged him or her. It is based on the idea that some human beings are better than others and you fear that you are not better than some other humans. You fear everyone might be better than you. You fear others will find out who you really are. Acceptance is just the opposite. Acceptance helps you find your way back to love—love of others and love of self. If you accept others as they are where they are, guess what? You may find that same acceptance just when you need it the most. Acceptance is loving others just as they are and loving yourself just the way that you are as well. The Dalai Lama said, "What is love? Love is the absence of judgment." That is beautiful.

Practice Self-Care

Acceptance of yourself brings you to a place of compassion for your own being. That compassion begins to blossom into wanting to take better care of yourself. This is what is called self-care. This might be a totally new concept for some of you but maybe not for others. As I may have mentioned before, I was an A+ people pleaser who took care of everyone else's needs first. My needs and wants were second to everyone else. It took me decades to begin to make myself a priority and take better care of myself and I'm still working on it.

As a rule, dolphins take care of themselves. No one else is going to do it for them. You know how they tell you at the beginning of a flight to put on your oxygen mask before you put it on your child. That is the core of the dolphin. As I like to say, you can't pour tea from an empty pot. If your pot of love and attention is empty for you, how can you pour out any more love or attention onto someone else's cup?

How do you practice self-care? Do you take the time to eat healthy foods, sleep, exercise, meditate, or whatever else you need to get centered and balanced? If you do, then your tank of love and energy is full and you can share it with others. You can take care of your kids if you are rested and ready to go. You can take care of aging parents if you have taken care of your own needs first. It's totally

OK to take care of your own needs before you start taking care of others. The only exception to this is occasionally with infants and small children. But don't neglect your own needs for too long. I've seen myself and too many other moms trying to do it all while not taking care of themselves. That leads to burnout, breakdowns, health challenges, and all sorts of bad things. Get a babysitter and go see a movie or take a nap. Ask someone to come clean your house or make your next meal and bring it over. Receive. Give yourself a break and take care of you.

I don't regret too many things in my life but I do regret not taking better care of myself when my son was just a baby. I needed to do a better job of taking care of me and I didn't. I think I had a lot of anger and resentment as a result which detracted from my ability to be 100% loving mom during those years.

Taking care of yourself means scheduling appointments to see the doctor, the hair stylist, the manicurist, the trainer, the yoga instructor, or whoever you need to see to take care of you in your body, mind, and spirit. No one else is going to do it. Take time to go to hear a lecture, a classical concert, take in a play, paint a picture, or sit outside at the park or the beach and read a book. This is your life. There is no do over. Take care of you now. Take care of all the parts of you including your creativity and playful side.

Then when you are being taken care of, you can take care of others with more love in your heart and a spring in your step. There will be no anger or resentment while you are fixing dinner or cleaning the house or taking the dog for a walk because you took care of you. And if you want your kids to start taking care of themselves and treating themselves well, be an example. If your kids see you never taking care of you, they will learn that's what adults do. This is related to setting boundaries. Dolphins are very good at boundaries and self-care is one of the important ones.

Self-Care Activities

List ways that you take care of yourself here so you can refer to this list to see if you are doing a good job of self-care. If you don't do a lot of self-care, then get busy and start making a list here of how you could start being a better job of taking care of yourself.

_____
_____
_____
_____
_____
_____
_____
_____
_____
_____
_____
_____
_____
_____
_____
_____
_____
_____
_____
_____
_____
_____
_____
_____

[12]

BE AUTHENTIC & OPEN

BRENÉ BROWN WROTE IN her book, **The Gifts of Imperfection: Let Go of Who You Think You're Supposed to Be and Embrace Who You Are**, "Authenticity is a collection of choices that we have to make every day. It's about the choice to show up and be real. The choice to be honest. The choice to let our true selves be seen." (Brown, The Gifts of Imperfection: Let Go of Who You Think You're Supposed to Be and Embrace Who You Are, 2010) How often do we think about being authentic? Do we know what this means?

All dolphins strive to be authentic by sharing openly who they are and let their true selves be seen by those around them. This stems from the previous dolphin behavior of acceptance of self and others. It's not that there is no filter but there is no denial of who you are. Filters are sometimes needed to be kind in our communication with others. Being blunt and direct is not the same as being authentic. Being authentic is standing up for yourself and what you believe to be true and acting on it. Again, this relates to knowing who you are and setting boundaries, which were described earlier. Being authentic is not playing manipulative games but clearly stating what is needed for you to thrive and continue. Being authentic is the choice to show up as real and honest.

This is about choosing love as your bottom line for how you show up in the world. If you choose fear as your bottom line, it could be because you are frightened to show up as your real self in this world. You might be afraid to be your wild, crazy, and not always logical self for fear of rejection. Let me tell you this. This world would be awfully boring if people chose to play small and not live their big authentic life by being their big authentic self. In Mahatma Gandhi's words, being authentic can lead to happiness, "Happiness is when what you think, what you say, and what you do are in perfect harmony." That's a perfect description of what it is like to live authentically.

Think about this quote for a minute. Being authentic is a pathway to happiness in this lifetime. Don't you want to be happy? When you fully and honestly express who you are, you experience a profound and deep sense of peace. It's a peace that is deep and wide and full of possibility. And when you feel that peace, you feel free. This peace and freedom allows you to relax into your life and whom you are bringing more happiness, and more peace and more freedom. It's a lovely merry-go-round that goes deeper and deeper with every turn.

For example, if you love science fiction like Star Trek (like I do), then proudly carry your Star Trek lunch box and communicator pin. If you love superheroes, then wear those Batman socks, Superman undershirt, or Wonder Woman Converse tennis shoes (I have these. They are cool. You should get some.). You can even wear a cape, if you like. Who cares? If this is who you are, be it. You'll be surprised at how many of us humans love it when someone just is themselves all out. You see it on those TV shows where they sing and dance and bring everything they have to the performance. We see that and we love it. It actually gives us all permission to be our authentic selves when someone else does it first. Be the one who does it first. It's a beautiful thing.

Practicing mindfulness and connecting to your own gas station in the sky instead of seeking out love, attention, energy, and approval from others all the time, opens up the space to be authentic. Do you see how these two are connected? When you aren't always seeking validation from others, you have more time to explore who you are, what you like, and finding ways to express who you are in the world. You don't care as much what other people think. You know you have a secret place to fill up your gas station and keep on going. This doesn't mean we don't need connection and love in our every day life. It just means that you don't need to spend so much time and energy filling up that gas tank by stealing energy from others. Do you see how that works? Find your freedom. Practice mindfulness and fill up your own gas tank. Then pave the way with your own authentic self.

As I mentioned, I have a pair of Converse tennis shoes with Wonder Woman on the sides. I love these shoes but do you know what? They sat in my closet for 8 years because I didn't feel free to wear them. I was hiding behind shoes that were boring and "acceptable." I didn't want to draw too much attention to myself so these shoes stayed in the closet. Then one day, I opened that closet and realized that my true self, my authentic self, would totally rock those shoes out in the world. I was stronger and more sure of myself and I wanted to put that on display.

So I took those shoes out and wore them and I've been wearing them several times a week for the past three years and you know what? I have never, ever had more compliments on my shoes than I have when I've worn the Wonder Woman tennis shoes. Everyone notices and everyone loves them. I used to think they were too bright or clown like or that my feet looked too big in them. When I chose to show up as my more authentic self down to the shoes, people liked it and commented on it. That was interesting. With that confidence in being who I truly am, I have begun to wear other things that really communicate who I am and again, I've gotten lots of compliments. I have an R2D2 scarf and a Star Wars t-shirt and they both get lots of attention. I feel great when I wear them and feel free to be my authentic self and to look for more ways to express who I am as an individual. It makes the world a much more interesting place when we all do that.

"Only the truth of who you are, if realized, will set you free." – Eckhart Tolle

Try to move yourself up on the measuring stick of authenticity because it is a sliding scale. Maybe you feel OK being authentic with some friends. Try to open up that world a little bigger. Grow your authenticity into every aspect of your life—what you wear, how you talk, what you eat, how you let others treat you, how you treat yourself, what you do for a living, who you love, how you love, and so on. Moving up the authenticity scale allows you more happiness, more peace, and more freedom. That's why you see so many dolphins jumping for joy out on the ocean. They feel all of that.

THE OPEN MIND

The old adage from Lord Thomas Robert Dewar who wrote "Minds are like parachutes. They only function when open." is still relevant today. And authenticity goes hand in hand with this openness and being humble. Openness or a beginner's mind allows more of the world to pass before your eyes allowing you to see what maybe you couldn't see before. It permits you to get to a greater point of view so you can see what is out there in the world. You want to see more so you get a greater understanding of the world around you and your place in it. You can see your own authentic self in reference to the world around you when you are in a state of openness. You are not judging, simply noticing where you are. Judgment shuts down the open mind.

Question everything as a dolphin as if you are that little four-year-old self who asks your mom why the sky is blue. Start with a beginner's mind and look at your own life with a fresh perspective. Why do you do what you do? Are you stuck in a rut? What if you chose to do one thing differently on this day? How would that open you up to new experiences? What if you did your hair differently or shook up your morning routine? What if you drove a different way to work or jogged on a different path? Or open yourself to questioning even larger things in your life. Look at it with new eyes.

Being open to new things and new ideas is crucial for a mammal like a dolphin. How do you think dolphins find new food sources or safe places to play? They explore. They keep an open mind. They listen to a distant cousin who said come try these fish over here and they did. Seeing the world through the eyes of a child can be transformative and so very helpful and that's what it means to have a beginner's mind.

Openness gives you access to new ideas, new ways of doing things and change. It is through change that you can develop yourself and give birth to success in mind, body, and spirit. Nolan Ryan, the famous baseball pitcher, once said, "Enjoying success requires the ability to adapt. Only by being open to change will you have a true opportunity to get the most from your talent." And it's true. How does a major league pitcher continue to get better? He is open to advice, tips, and his own curiosity on how to do things better. He asks himself questions about what he did wrong and what he could do better and what can he do differently or just try to see if it works. That kind of attitude leads to greatness in one's self and in how one shows up in the world. Along with that sense of openness, comes humility. They are forever bound up together. Because when you ask questions, you automatically come from a place of humility because you are uncertain of the answer. In asking the question, you admit you don't know the answer. You are open to whatever answer comes your way. It is from this childlike humility and the ability to ask questions that some of our most amazing scientific discoveries and technological advances have been made.

Charles Filmore, founder of the Unity Church, wrote "It is the childlike mind that finds the kingdom." I can't help but think that

Steve Jobs took this approach when developing the iPhone and the iPad. Something like that had never existed before in our world. He must have had a childlike wonder to think up the possibility of such a device. That's genius and we all have access to it. You have to have a sense of openness to new ideas to allow ideas to collect and simmer and then explode into the world. That's the only way those new technological innovations could be born with questioning and openness and a child's eyes.

Steve Jobs once said, "Don't let the noise of other's opinions drown out your own inner voice. And most important, have the courage to follow your heart and intuition. They somehow already know what you truly want to become. Everything else is secondary." Be open, ask questions, and be authentically you. The world is in desperate need of what you have to offer.

[13]

Letting Go & Trusting the Universe

THERE IS A POINT in a dolphin's life when he or she has picked up and practiced all the other behaviors and now it's down to letting go and trusting that it will all work out for the best. This is crucial. One of life's most important lessons is that we can't control everything. What we can control are our thoughts, words, intentions, actions, and reactions. If we have dedicated ourselves to setting good intentions, staying mindful, and being responsible for keeping our energy up, then we must let go and trust the universe to come through with the rest.

About three years ago, my husband was suddenly let go as part of a giant layoff at a large company here in San Diego. My husband is the primary wage earner in our family and his job gives us our health insurance, which, as most of you know, is a huge thing in the United States. My husband had worked for several years to get a position at this prestigious company and had been there for only nine months when he was laid off. He came home from work that day just devastated. Many of his co-workers were beyond devastated as many of them had been employed by this company for 10, 15, or even 20 years and were let go with little notice. They were given nice compensation packages but still, it was hard.

I know I had a challenge ahead of me as did my husband. My challenge was to hold our family together and begin setting intentions for a new job with good pay and good health insurance that would come quickly for my husband. I began visualizing my husband happy with his new job and settling in and meeting new co-workers. I visualized a large paycheck and good health insurance coverage. I pictured this happening quickly and easily. I set intentions and read them out loud after I meditated. I stayed positive. My husband did his part by freshening up his résumé and project portfolio. He began poring over job boards and asking his friends and past co-workers for leads on any openings that might be a good fit for him. My husband was given three months pay and health insurance coverage in which to find a new job without us having to dip into savings or start paying out of pocket for healthcare.

My husband was laid off in June. He took a few weeks off to just relax and sit with this new realization that his life was changing. We spent time together as a family since my son was out for summer vacation from school. After that, my husband began his job search in earnest sending out resumés and job applications. We had already planned a trip to Zion National Park in Utah in early August and we decided to go anyway despite my husband's lack of a job. Our reservations were in place and we needed a little recreational time in nature. This turned out to be perfect timing. My husband had done as much as he could sending out feelers and emails regarding job possibilities so when we left for Las Vegas (the starting point for our journey into Utah), we just let go. We decided to have fun and try not to think about it. We drove up to Zion right after a buffet lunch in Las Vegas eager to enjoy the natural setting. We loved our hotel just outside the national park and enjoyed a swim looking up at the red rock cliffs above us. We had to let go and trust that the universe would unfold just as it should for our best and highest good.

We did let go. We breathed into the beauty of nature. We had a great time taking the bus deep into the valley of Zion and hiking around watching deer and squirrels. We saw big horn sheep and even a tarantula. We experienced the deep peace of this magical place. On the third day of our trip, my husband received a request for a phone interview from a large company who had received his application. They wanted to have a phone interview in two days.

We would be in St. George, Utah, by then staying at a beautiful vacation rental house we rented for a few nights on our way back to Las Vegas. That would be an ideal place for a phone interview. I could take our son to the pool while my husband had a comfortable place to conduct business in private with wifi and cell service. My husband set it up and had a very successful interview. Within three weeks of that call, my husband began his new job on a Monday morning. The health insurance at the old employer ran out the Friday before.

My intentions for having us be cared for and getting a new job quickly and easily all worked out. The universe unfolded just as it should. It all worked out with grace and ease and my husband got to spend the entire summer with our son and me. It actually couldn't have worked out much better. Do you see how that worked? We had to let go and let the universe unfold. But we weren't passive about it either. We set our intentions, we visualized, we kept positive, and we took action (sending out résumés, emails, and making phone calls).

It's almost as if you have to distract yourself to let go completely. The trip to Zion completely distracted us from the stressful dance of trying to get a new job. This worked to our advantage in this case. The letting go allowed the universe to unfold for our best and highest good. My husband still has this job today and we are thankful.

[14]

Cooperation Over Competition

RECENTLY, I WAS SITTING near some Moms while watching my son's baseball team play. One of the moms had hurt her ankle while playing tennis that morning. The other mom asked her if the doubles team she was playing against used her hurt ankle to their advantage. She added that she would have totally done that so she could win. I know it was just meaningless banter but the conversation jarred me enough to wonder about what motivates me. I don't have a competitive bone in my body. I just never have.

After that conversation, I was starting to think that maybe something is wrong with me. Maybe the competitive spirit is what I'm missing and could explain why I have not become a multi-millionaire yet. I started to think I was weird because I would never use someone's injury to gain an advantage. I would probably feel sorry for them and take it easy on them so we could all have fun in the end.

The situation made me ponder competition and cooperation. And it's not that I think competition is bad just that I think cooperation is better. When you are playing a game, I understand competition. It can make it fun. It can help you try harder and do better than your best. I just never felt its effects very much when I was playing a sport or competing for anything really. My son, on the other hand, is very competitive and it drives him to get better and better and that's great. But I always felt a bit different in this regard. I could never scrounge up a competitive edge to outdo someone or beat anyone. I love cooperative videogames like "Little Big Planet" that I used to play with my son. You actually work together to move forward in the game. For example, I would stay and stand on a button to push my son up an elevator so he could then open a door for both of us and we could move forward. It was fun.

These games are not nearly as popular as the competitive ones although there has been a push to create more cooperative games for kids in recent years. Still, in our culture, it's all about the individual winning. Cooperation is not always rewarded. I didn't feel comfortable wading into the conversation with those two moms, as I wasn't sure what to say. Our society places such importance on winning so do I pretend that matters to me? I didn't know where I stood on the subject so I walked back to the baseball game, sat down, and watched.

From a much broader cultural perspective then, I asked myself is competition such a good thing? Is it OK that our culture thrives on competition and we think the winner is the one with the most toys and the largest mansion? For most people, I think competition is probably on a sliding scale depending on the type of situation and the consequences. But what would a dolphin think about competition? I think they would see a place for it if it brought them joy. Maybe they have underwater races or see how high each other can jump out of the water. I have no idea. But then what would a dolphin do if one of the dolphins in his pod were hurt? What would a dolphin do if there was only one big fish and he and another dolphin were sizing it up for dinner? What would happen then?

In thinking about this topic, I remembered reading Lynne McTaggart's book, **The Bond**, which is all about re-examining

Darwin's theory of survival of the fittest to see if it still fits. McTaggart makes the case that we and our animal friends are hard wired for cooperation, not competition. In her introduction for **The Bond**, she writes, "The Bond ultimately posits an alternative future in which a new paradigm for living in partnership and connection replaces the metaphor for battle." (McTaggart, The Bond: How to Fix Your Falling-Down World, 2011, p. XXVI)

McTaggart provides summaries of research about intention relating to quantum physics and how mirror neurons show how closely we relate to each other. She even cites research from Columbia University that of 655 stroke patients, "those patients who were socially isolated were twice as likely to have another stroke within five years compared with those who had strong social relationships." (McTaggart, The Bond: How to Fix Your Falling-Down World, 2011, p. 80) I was astonished that even being a member of a group could result in greater health and wellness and that social isolation had devastating effects.

I think about two of my grandparents. My mother's father who lived alone in Kansas City, MO was a part of many groups especially his church. He taught Sunday school to the seniors there and lived to be a few days shy of 90 years old. He was entirely self-sufficient living in his own home taking care of himself until the end even though he had diabetes the last fifty years of his life.

My father's mother, on the other hand, lived alone in an apartment isolated from groups and only had family come visit occasionally. She never learned to drive and found it difficult to walk places. I have to think she was very lonely. I wish I knew then what I know now. Maybe we could have made other arrangements for her. She ended up with dementia and lived in a senior assisted living establishment until she died a few years later. I am so thankful that my parents, both still alive and healthy, are active socially and my Mom regularly attends fitness classes with friends. My Dad regularly golfs and loves talking up his fellow players. I will definitely keep this in mind as I grow older. I need to stay in social groups not only because it provides a means of connection but also for the health benefits inherent in that connection.

How can we think we are not wired for cooperation over competition when faced with some of this research? McTaggart continues "The need to move beyond the boundaries of ourselves as individuals and to bond with a group is so primordial and necessary to human beings that it remains the key determinant of whether we remain healthy or get ill, even whether we live or die." (McTaggart, The Bond: How to Fix Your Falling-Down World, 2011, p. 83) How powerful is that?

No wonder prisons consider solitary confinement the worst possible punishment they can mete out. I was so glad I reread this book, as there is so much material and research to be happy about. I liked being reminded that we are wired for connection and cooperation. When our Western society learns this (or remembers this) and embraces this as a cultural norm, the world will be a much different place. I'm not saying that competition is bad. In fact, competition can bring people together and be a source for joy and flow and teamwork (think baseball or soccer). I just want us to notice that we might do better as a species if we put cooperation ahead of competition.

There are many examples of cooperation in nature that we can point to for further inspiration. A clear example is the V formation of birds. Scientists have been able to verify that the V formation is a cooperative effort of the birds to save energy. (Wald, 2014) Researchers studied ibises and logged data on the backs of these birds to determine if the V formation does truly save energy. It's remarkable that these birds know just where to position themselves with pinpoint accuracy in regards to each other to optimize their community output of energy for maximum aerodynamics. They work as a group to fly better and more economically. That is amazing and shows true cooperation.

I read of another example recently where plants issue warnings to other plants. Back in the early 1980s, a zoologist, David Rhoades, was discovering how plants defend themselves and what he found made a lot of people doubt his research. He found that plants can create and send out chemical signals to neighboring plants to let them know they are under attack. Then those neighbors secrete a chemical that makes their foliage less appetizing for those who are attacking the original plant.

What we used to think about plants being passive prey is just not true. They have defense mechanisms that are sophisticated and that help their neighbors survive. We call this cooperation but never expected to find it in plants. Rhoades was discredited for his work but more researchers like Ted Farmer and Clarence Ryan came along. They studied sagebrush and noted how they used an airborne organic chemical to ward off insects and even sent this chemical out to warn other species like tomato plants. The tomato plants then produced a proteinase inhibitor that disrupts the digestion systems of insects thereby protecting themselves from an attack. (MacGown, 2013) Why did the sagebrush bother doing this? It was secreting this chemical to save another species? Cooperation wins over competition even in plant species. That is very interesting.

I have always loved dolphins. When I went to UCLA my freshman year, the one poster I took was of dolphins. It was a photo by Talbot. Dolphins live in pods that cooperate for feeding, looking after their young, and watching for predators. Their way of life depends on cooperating with each other so it's a good fit for my metaphor in this book. While doing some research, I came across this story about humans and dolphins cooperating in Brazil. (Roman, 2013) The fishermen in Laguna, Brazil have been cooperating with many of the resident dolphins for 120 years to catch fish.

On a small beach called Tesoura, fishermen gather when they see the dorsal fins of helpful dolphins. A fisherman will splash his net into the water so the dolphin would know where he is and then the dolphin races for the shore driving fish towards the net. The fisherman gets a nice big tainha, or local mullet, trapped in his net quickly and easily with the help of the dolphin. The dolphin wasn't competing; it was cooperating, with the fisherman. It is not clear if this helps the dolphin in some way. Maybe in the chaos of the chase, the dolphin can snatch a larger, quicker fish than he normally could but it's difficult to know for sure. But these fishermen know the value of the dolphin's cooperation and don't even bother throwing their nets out there unless they see the familiar sight of the dorsal fin just offshore.

"Competition has been shown to be useful up to a certain point and no further, but cooperation, which is the thing we must strive for today, begins where competition leaves off." –Franklin D. Roosevelt

Maybe that's the key. When competition leaves off, we can come together in cooperation. We value competition for what it can bring us but then we must move past it into a space of cooperation that leads us to even greater gains. Wayne Dyer wrote, "When you move into a spiritual approach to life you begin to see yourself as connected to everyone and everything, and competition is replaced by something called cooperation." (Dyer, 2001) If we go back to our first underlying assumption that we are all connected, wouldn't it be better if we then undertook cooperation over competition? We'll move forward with more grace and ease if we work together.

Even Albert Einstein underscored the importance of cooperation when he wrote, "Today we must abandon competition and secure cooperation. This must be the central fact in all our considerations of international affairs; otherwise we face certain disaster." (Rowe, 2007, p. 383) This needs to be the way we interact with each other as the basis of our world culture. We are on one planet and we need to cooperate for the good of all of us. We are all each other's brothers and sisters sharing one resource (i.e. this planet) so doesn't cooperation make more sense?

[15]

A World of Dolphins

A Community or Pod of Dolphins

WE ARE ALL CONNECTED. I'm back to one of the underlying principles for this book. We are in a giant herd of many, many pods of dolphins. Our pod matters. The health and happiness of our pod matters. We are each responsible for the energy and emotions we bring to our pod and to the collective herd. I found the research reported in the book, **Connected**, to be fascinating in supporting this notion.

Christakis and Fowler report "We found that each happy friend a person has increases that person's probability of being happy by about 9 percent. Each unhappy friend decreases it by 7 percent." And then those percentages can be affected by proximity. The authors go on "We found that when a friend who lives less than a mile away becomes happy, it can increase the probability that you are happy by 25 percent." (Christakis & Fowler, 2009, p. 53) Wow. This even applies to next-door neighbors who also play a role in your happiness. A happy community really matters.

We are all ripples in a pond. If we take responsibility for our ripple and make it a heart-centered one, what will the effects be on our pod? What about within the larger pod of our community? What about the world as a whole? So we are back to the idea that change begins with you. I hope you can see that now and how important that is. You matter, more so than you'll ever know. Find your heart-centered way. Maintain and be responsible for your energy so you can find happiness daily and raise up those around you. It's beyond important at this point.

My Vision

I have this vision and my intuition keeps pushing me to share it as often as possible with as many people as possible. And the words of John Lennon keep popping into my head every time I think about it, "You may think I'm a dreamer but I'm not the only one." So, here's my dream of what the world might look like if we were all living as dolphins most of the time. And yes, I am a dreamer but we need dreamers in this world to keep hope alive. I will just keep on dreaming.

The dream begins with a woman we'll call Diana who is going to the hairstylist for an appointment. Her hairstylist greets her warmly with a hug. She has been doing Diana's hair for many years. Diana sits in the chair and does not know exactly what she wants to do with her hair but knows she wants a change. She decides to trust her stylist to cut and color as her intuition guides her. She places complete faith in her friend, the hairstylist. The hairstylist is excited and recently bought a new shade of hair color with Diana in mind and now she'll get a chance to use it. She also had looked through a hairstyle magazine recently, which gave her a new idea for a hairstyle that would suit perfectly.

Now she got into the flow of coloring and cutting hair consulting with Diana throughout the appointment. Diana looks in the mirror at the final reveal and LOVES the cut and color. It's everything she wanted but didn't know how to express. She tips her stylist generously and leaves feeling fabulous.

Diana is now going to meet her friend Victoria for lunch down the street. She walks there smiling and humming a tune so happy with her new look. On the way there, she sees a policeman laughing with a pair of teenage boys outside the liquor store. The policeman had been meditating before his shift and setting intention for a peaceful community with no arrests. And during this time, his intuition kept showing him this particular liquor store like he needed to go there on his rounds this morning. So, the policeman followed his hunch and poked his head in just as two teenage boys were getting ready to steal a magazine and some candy from the unaware owner behind the counter.

The policeman came in smiling and shared a story with these boys about how he got caught one time trying to shoplift a record from the music store when he was about their age. The policeman who caught him taught him about respect, integrity, and the law. And it was that experience that drew him to being a policeman as a profession. Sharing this vulnerable story created a connection between the policeman and the boys. The owner realizing what had happened decided to treat them all to a drink and a candy bar, which they were sharing outside when Diana walked by.

Victoria was waiting for Diana just outside The Lemon Tree Café. They greeted each other warmly and went inside to sit by the window. Earlier that morning, the waitress had made some peach mango iced tea, which was unusual. She just felt an urge to make it today so she followed through on that. When the waitress came over for their drink order, Victoria asked what kind of iced tea they had and when she heard that it was peach mango, she was delighted. She and Diana both ordered it. The waitress was pleased that her intuition had been correct and she was lucky that the owner encouraged her to practice using her intuition as much as possible in her responsibilities at the café.

The chef at The Lemon Tree Café used only fresh, organic produce because the energy of it was fabulous. During his mindfulness practice that morning, he had set intentions that he would get what he needed at the market to make gorgeous and delicious food for his customers that day. He envisioned all his customers absolutely delighted with their meals leaving large tips. He went to the market early that morning for some needed supplies and found himself obsessed with small, multi-colored tomatoes in orange, yellow, and red hues. He bought some along with cilantro for a special sauce he didn't usually make. He just felt compelled to buy it.

Diana ordered the salmon plate special with a cilantro sauce while Victoria ordered a grilled chicken salad with baby tomatoes. The chef saw the order and smiled to himself. He could see that his intuition was right again. The cilantro was perfect with the salmon and the colorful tomatoes would be a lovely addition to the grilled chicken salad. He loved it when his food was beautiful and tasty. He was feeling in the flow and happily prepared the fresh, tasty food for these customers. The ladies were so pleased they left a generous tip and the entire restaurant was filled with happy customers and a great energy that day.

Victoria and Diana had to cross the street to get to their cars in the parking lot of the library. A young girl who had been running with earphones on was next to them and began to enter the intersection before the light turned green while looking down at her phone. Diana reached out and stopped the girl just as a car went whizzing by. The girl was surprised and said "Thanks." The ladies went their separate ways. Diana went home to write the novel she was working on while Victoria got ready to teach her next yoga class. They would meet back later at the park near the library for a community picnic to raise money for the new town meditation center to be built at the park.

Final Note

And these scenarios could go on and on. This may sound like the town of Mayberry in the Andy Griffith Show (for those of you old enough to remember that) or life on the show "Leave it to Beaver" but with a New Age twist. But I maintain that this is possible. There is a synchronicity and flow when life is lived like a dolphin with a pod of other dolphins. There is heart-centeredness, mindfulness, and intuition plus a desire to help the community be better and stronger. People work together and live together in peaceful relation to one another. There is harmony. This is my vision. I have been fortunate enough to experience this flow of dolphin like energy while running spiritual events where people came together beautifully to make the event happen. But it does not happen often and the energy does not always stay up. You have to take specific actions to keep the energy up and flowing but maybe I'll leave that for the next book.

There are advanced dolphin behaviors that I have not covered here. When you learn more about energy and begin to be able to feel it and work with it in your relationship to yourself, you can begin to share it with others and that is a beautiful thing. You can send energy for healing or to uplift someone. You can energetically protect and uplift places and events. You can place your children in a bubble of protective energy. There are many ways in which dolphins continue to define and strengthen their work with energy but at least in this book, you now have the groundwork to get started on this journey of being the dolphin.

Works Cited

Bernier, M., Thienot, E., Codron, R., & Fournier, J. F. (2009). Mindfulness and Acceptance Approaches in Sport Performance. Journal of Clinical Sports Psychology, 4, 320-333.

Breathnach, S. B. (1995). Simple Abundance (1st Edition ed.). New York, NY, USA: Warner Books.

Brown, B. (2011, 02 21). Author Brené Brown Discusses Embracing Our Ordinariness. Retrieved 12 8, 2015, from Huffington Post: http://www.huffingtonpost.com/martha-rosenberg/embracing-our-ordinariness_b_802808.html

Brown, B. (2015). Rising Strong. New York, NY, USA: Spiegel & Grau.

Brown, B. (2010). The Gifts of Imperfection: Let Go of Who You Think You're Supposed to Be and Embrace Who You Are. Center City, MN, USA: Hazelden Publishing.

Childre, D., Martin, H., & Beech, D. (1999). The HeartMath Solution. New York, NY, USA: HarperCollins Publishers.

Christakis, N. A., & Fowler, J. H. (2009). Connected: The Surprising Power of Our Social Networks and How They Shape Our Lives. New York, NY, USA: Little, Brown and Company.

Csikszentmihalyi, M. (1990). Flow: The Psychology of Optimal Experience (1st Edition ed.). New York, NY, USA: Harper & Row.

Dooley, M. (2011). Leveraging the Universe. New York, NY, USA: Atria Books.

Dyer, D. W. (2001, 09). PBS Member Drive. Concord Church, MA, USA: PBS.

Einstein, A. (1950). Letter to Robert Marcus.

Gordhamer, S. (2011, 04 15). The Lakers Meditate? Retrieved 11 29, 2015, from Mindful.org: http://www.mindful.org/the-lakers-meditate/#

Kabat-Zinn, J. (2005). Coming To Our Senses: Healing Ourselves and the World Through Mindfulness (First ed.). New York, NY, USA: Hyperion.

Kee, Y., & Wang, C. J. (2008). Relationships between mindfulness, flow dispositions and mental skills adoption: A cluster analytic approach . Psychology of Sport and Exercise , 393-411.

Lee, H. (2015). To Kill A Mockingbird. New York, NY, USA: Harper.

MacGown, K. (2013, 12 20). How Plants Secretly Talk To Each Other. Retrieved 11 25, 2015, from Wired.com: http://www.wired.com/2013/12/secret-language-of-plants/

McCraty, R. (2004). Research. Retrieved 11 03, 2015, from HeartMath: https://www.heartmath.org/research/research-library/energetics/energetic-heart-bioelectromagnetic-communication-within-and-between-people/

McTaggart, L. (2011). The Bond: How to Fix Your Falling-Down World. New York, NY, USA: FREE PRESS Simon & Schuster.

McTaggart, L. (2008). The Field: The Quest for the Secret Force of the Universe. New York, NY, USA: HarperCollins.

McTaggart, L. (2007). The Intention Experiment. New York, NY, USA: Simon & Schuster.

Redfield, J. (1993). The Celestine Prophecy: An Adventure. New York, NY, USA: Warner Books.

Roman, J. (2013, 01 31). Fishing with Dolphins. Retrieved 01 28, 2016, from Slate.com: http://www.slate.com/articles/health_and_science/science/2013/01/fishing_with_dolphins_symbiosis_between_humans_and_marine_mammals_to_catch.html

Rowe, D. E. (2007). Einstein on Politics. Princeton, NJ, USA: Princeton University Press.

Ruiz, D. M. (1997). The Four Agreements: A Toltec Wisdom Book. San Rafael, CA, USA: Amber-Allen Publishing.

Schawbel, D. (2013, 04 21). Brené Brown: How Vulnerability Can Make Our Lives Better. Retrieved 10 24, 2015, from Forbes.com: http://www.forbes.com/sites/danschawbel/2013/04/21/brene-brown-how-vulnerability-can-make-our-lives-better/#2ae1401960ba

Schoeberlein, D., & Sheth, S. (2009). Mindful Teaching and Teaching Mindfulness: A Guide for Anyone Who Teaches Anything. Somerville, MA, USA: Wisdom Publications.

Tyson, N. d. (n.d.). Quotes from Neil deGrasse Tyson. Retrieved 04 19, 2016, from BrainyQuote: http://www.brainyquote.com/quotes/quotes/n/neildegras531166.html

Wald, C. (2014, 01 15). Precision Formation Flight Astounds Scientists. Retrieved 10 18, 2015, from Nature.com:: http://www.nature.com/news/precision-formation-flight-astounds-scientists-1.14537

Weiner, B. (1985). Human Motivation. New York, NY, USA: Springer-Verlag.

Wilson, R. (2014, 09 10). Wildlife Energy: Survival of the Fittest. Retrieved 07 15, 2015, from Nature.com: http://www.nature.com/news/wildlife-energy-survival-of-the-fittest-1.15857

Zondervan. (2010). Holy Bible, King James Version. New York, NY, USA: Zondervan.

ABOUT THE AUTHOR

Melinda McDonald Pajak resides in Southern California with her husband and son. Her love of learning continues to drive her to seek wisdom and happiness on her journey. Her hope is that the people in the world strive every day to live more like dolphins. This would be a good thing.

Visit melindapajak.com to learn more.

"Never forget that you are one of a kind. Never forget that if there weren't any need for you in all of your uniqueness to be on this earth, you wouldn't be here in the first place. And never forget, no matter how overwhelming life's challenges and problems seem to be, that one person can make a difference in the world. In fact, it is always because of one person that all the changes that matter in the world come about. So be that one person."

-R. Buckminster Fuller

www.ingramcontent.com/pod-product-compliance
Lightning Source LLC
Chambersburg PA
CBHW050533300426
44113CB00012B/2075